THE DECADE AFTER

THE DECADE AFTER

~~SURVIVING~~ THRIVING AFTER DIVORCE

Toyin M. Falusi MD

ISBN-13: 9781974133369
ISBN-10: 1974133362
Library of Congress Control Number: 2017912183
CreateSpace Independent Publishing Platform
North Charleston, South Carolina

Survive: To continue to live or exist, especially in spite of danger or hardship.
Synonyms: Remain alive, live, make it, hold on, pull through.

Thrive: Grow or develop well or vigorously.
Synonyms: flourish, prosper, bloom, blossom, do well, advance, succeed.

To Oluwatosin (TosTos) and Oluwafunmilola (Fumsie): You inspire me daily and make me want to be the best person I can be. I love you with all my heart, and no matter how old you are, you will always be my baby girls.

CONTENTS

PREFACE

WHEN YOU ARE going through a divorce, it feels like you are stumbling through a never-ending dark tunnel, and you have no idea how you're going to get through or what it's going to look like on the other side. For the last few years, friends have told me to start a blog, write a book, and share tips on how to successfully navigate the single-mom thing. I've had this book in my head for a while, and I'm thrilled that it's finally on paper. I got divorced at thirty-five after nine and a half years of marriage, when my daughters were six and seven. It was rough, challenging, and filled with a flurry of emotions, but time is amazing! The saying "time heals all wounds" is true, and my journey is living, breathing proof of that. Also true is that we should choose how we spend our precious time and who we spend it with as we heal from a divorce.

I wrote this book twelve years after my divorce to share that being on the other side can be fabulous and that you will get through the divorce process intact. I won't go into the details of who did what in my marriage or why it ended. This is not that book! This book is about my decade post divorce and the path to growth and raising well-adjusted kids. Here I am a decade later, better than ever, and my children are young women who are almost out of the house.

I can honestly say that they are smart, savvy, considerate, compassionate, well-adjusted young women with high emotional IQs. They have a great relationship with their dad and have navigated the children-of-divorced-parents thing quite well.

This is not a how-to manual or professional advice from an expert. It's a divorced mom sharing her thoughts, tips, and ups and downs with friends. It's about finding peace in a stressful or stress-prone situation. This may not be entirely applicable to a mom who's single by choice and does not want a co-parent or even a divorced mom whose ex is no longer involved in the children's lives, but if any of the things I found useful during my journey resonate with you, I am thrilled to bits. If you read sections and nod in agreement or laugh out loud or sigh in remembrance or pick up the phone and call someone to share with, you've made me even happier. I also hope that those who know or love a single mom read this and get insight into our hectic, amazing, sometimes stressful, wonderful lives. It's time to change that old, tired stereotype and retire the myth of the miserable divorced single mom. Fasten your seat belts, and join me on the ride twelve years in.

Enjoy.

CHAPTER 1

RANDOM MUSINGS

A FEW THINGS BEFORE WE DELVE IN

I AM A complicated woman with a simple life. I derive immense pleasure from the simple things around me. I am serious and no-nonsense at work, but I also like to laugh and have fun. I delight in being outside enjoying nature, and I love learning new things. I consider myself an introvert who also likes being around people. I enjoy company but crave and relish alone time to replenish my stores. Books make me happy, and bookstores are my havens. I like to visit new places, though I am not a fan of flying. I love a good joke and think I can tell a few good ones. I am a loyal friend and march to my own tune. I love to dance, and I can't sing. I suck at remembering names. I am a nerd and carry my nerd card proudly. My perfect Friday night is in my bed with a good book and a glass of wine by nine. (Yeah, I know—boring! And nothing like the glamorous divorcées on Bravo or VH1.) I am a strong woman. I am a daughter; I am a sister; I am a friend; I am a mother. I am a physician. I am American by birth, but I am also Nigerian. I am a hybrid of two wonderful cultures. I have amazing children who are straddling two cultures and acing life. I was a wife. The woman I am is not defined by my divorce, and you are not defined by yours. You are awesome, and that is more than enough.

I have a career that I love and consider a calling. I also have a steady income, which made it easier to transition into being a single mom. My co-parent and I had a parenting agreement, and he paid child support willingly. I say this because some women may point out, and rightly so, that it's easy to be Zen and take things in stride when your lifestyle is fine. What if I have to go back to work? What if I have to work more? What about childcare? What if I have to downsize? What if I want children? What if I want more children? What if my ex doesn't keep up his side of the bargain? What if…? I understand this, but as I said earlier, this is not a how-to book. It's about sharing tips I learned on my personal journey after my marriage was over.

There are things you can do to grow as a woman and prioritize the children regardless of your circumstances. I will use humor (my go-to coping mechanism), and you will see examples of and analogies to medicine in this book. I have been a physician for longer than I have been a mother and for much longer than I was a wife, so this is my comfort zone.

In medicine, while radiation therapy can be unpleasant, it is needed in many instances to fight cancer cells. It can be rough, and the radiation-oncology experts take special care to minimize damage to the normal surrounding tissues. This minimizes the short- and long-term side effects of a successful treatment. While divorce is not cancer, in both cases you must go through a hard time to reach a successful outcome, and it's important to protect the surrounding tissues so the postmarriage-divorce-survivor version of you emerges stronger and better. You don't want to look back a decade after your divorce to realize you are wiser and stronger but the poor kids have been damaged significantly, even irreversibly, by the process. As mothers, we need to take extra care of the normal surrounding tissues (our children) during this often unpleasant process.

It's not always easy, and many days, especially early on, you will miss having an in-house partner and co-parent. I am not just talking about sex on demand or a warm body in bed. Sometimes you just want another adult to share with, complain to, or bond with after a long day at work or at home taking care of the children. You may also sometimes wish you didn't have to schedule the oil change, get the car washed, replace light bulbs, take out trash (assuming your spouse did these chores; mine did), or be the good cop and the bad cop at the same time.

My moments usually came when it was time for car maintenance or filling the car with gas (hate doing it) or when I had to split the parent-teacher meetings and run around like a chicken missing its head. Seeing couples walking down the hall or splitting up to divide and conquer made me miss being part of a couple. After the parent-teacher meetings, the fact that they were in the same school, doing fabulously, and acing the classes was my treat.

Always find the positive, no matter what, and remember that just because you miss something (your spouse) does not mean you want it back. We miss familiarity, stability, and predictability, but sometimes we have no choice. Once you realize that, it's time to make the best of that transition.

The first few months and years one and two are really hard. When faced with adversity, most of us go into one of two modes—sad or mad. I went the mad route, which fueled me and kept me going. I felt like the sad route was ineffective and paralyzing—I didn't have time to be sad. I had to be supermom and superdoctor and do this without skipping a beat. I didn't allow myself to be sad. The adrenaline (or mad hormones, as I like to call them) spurred me on to sell our house, buy a new house, and move the kids to a new school all in a few months without missing a beat or a day at work. I prided myself on the fact that I wasn't wallowing in self-pity and was moving on in a speedy, take-charge manner. However, not allowing myself to be sad also had its downsides. It made me mad for much longer—not mad in a lash-out way, but mad in an "I don't need anyone; I can do it all by myself" way. It's OK to be sad, but I learned that much later. When relationships end, they should be mourned and not brushed off or repressed. Going through the phases of loss is important for you and for the children, and I discuss that in detail later in the book.

In medicine, when we give people a devastating diagnosis and they immediately shake it off and are spurred to action, we are happy that they're ready to get the treatment plan going, but we secretly wonder if they understood what was just said. I've had multidisciplinary meetings and gotten mental-health counselors involved when the reaction to a diagnosis and process seemed inappropriate. Sometimes people in shock or denial can look like they are in the acceptance stage, and I may not find out until much later that that they never accepted the diagnosis. This explains how, after months of treatments and interactions with many physicians, a patient will say, "I didn't know I was that sick," or, "No one ever told me it was that bad."

As I went through my divorce, I felt that being too sad was a sign of weakness, and I must confess that I looked down on sad women in movies and on TV shows (and sometimes in real life). I couldn't relate to women who seemed to spiral into despair over a man. As a young woman, I was never one to despair over a breakup or wallow over a guy, and with two young girls who needed me to be there, I definitely was not about to wallow. That being said, it is natural to be sad, sometimes cripplingly sad, after a marriage ends. If you skip the natural mourning process, it can delay the healing or cause an unexpected implosion or explosion later. Fortunately, I didn't implode or explode, but my anger made me tougher and my shell harder. I felt I had to be present all the time with my kids and do it all, but it's important to be kind to yourself and be sad if you need to. (And you need to!)

I was married to my college and medical-school best friend whom I loved dearly. When the marriage ended, I was good at being mad but not so good at being sad.

There are, of course, many other emotions in addition to sad and mad, and you will often cycle through these, sometimes in a single day. The chapters that follow outline how the process, situations, and emotions evolved for me over the first decade postdivorce.

I mentioned that I am American by birth; however, I was born to Nigerian parents, was raised in Nigeria, and have lived in America for the last twenty-three years. Straddling two cultures can be difficult, even as an adult. It's difficult enough raising bicultural kids, but being a divorced Nigerian mom is particularly challenging, especially for someone who was married to a fellow Nigerian like I was. For Nigerians, divorce is not commonplace and is frowned upon. I had no friends who were divorced, and the idea that 40 to 50 percent of marriages ended in divorce was an abstract, even mythical statistic—definitely not my reality. In my family, work life, and community, I did not have a single family member or friend who was divorced. More than a decade later, it is still a tiny group.

A medical-school classmate came to Chicago for a conference in 2016 (eleven years after my divorce and twenty-three years postgraduation), and he met up with four of his classmates, including me and my ex, for dinner. The four of us who lived in Chicago were divorced, and our classmate, who lived in Nigeria, was married. We learned from him that none of our classmates in Nigeria were divorced. I wondered—were they all happily married? Probably not. But they were all still married. This is the reality for many women straddling two cultures, and it does not provide us with many people to bounce things off. I hope by writing this book and sharing my experiences and unique perspective, I can help other women going through the process.

In the next few chapters, I will draw on my experiences and share insights, practical lessons, and tips that I picked up along the way. I will discuss issues regarding you and the children; you and your co-parent; how others react to your divorce and how you relate to them; and most important, how to grow through the process. You will see examples from medicine because I love medicine and can apply it to my personal life. I have been an infectious-diseases physician for almost twenty years, and I have learned so much from my patients who are living and aging with HIV. I have found that the patients who are not only surviving but thriving are the ones who embody many of the things I will talk about in this book. They accept the HIV diagnosis and look for ways to live to the fullest. They know it is not a death sentence and refuse to stay stuck in the why-me mode. They are proactive; they do their research and keep up with their appointments and medications. They strive to get better daily; they engage their support system and use resources available to them. They don't sweat the small stuff and are in tune with their bodies. They understand the importance of caring for their bodies and taking time to renew and repair. They make time to give back by volunteering in the clinic and support others who are newly diagnosed or struggling with the diagnosis. They realize that no matter how they got infected or whatever their age, gender, socioeconomic status or sexual orientation, they all want the same thing—to live healthy, productive lives and enjoy life to the fullest.

I will also use analogies and quotes from Stephen Covey's book, *The 7 Habits of Highly Effective People*. This book, one of his many inspirational books, is one of my all-time favorites—an oldie but goodie and a must-read for any adult. The seven habits fall into private victories, public victories, and renewal and are highly applicable to any situation, including how you approach and live your life postdivorce. As Covey states, "If you do something often enough, it becomes a habit." That means with time, effort, skill, and the will to do so, we can change bad habits and create new narratives. Wherever you live and whatever your nationality, it's time to change the narrative about the miserable or thirsty divorcée.

Most people, including me, go into marriage hoping for forever and happy-ever-after and do not have a divorce agenda, but once it happens, the resolve to go on and thrive is imperative. We move from our independent place as single women to a state of interdependence during marriage. When the marriage ends, we are plunged into a free fall—a place with so much uncertainty and fear. I hope you read every sentence in this book and realize that the postmarriage phase is a time of growth, new beginnings, and the launch of the new and improved you.

THE IMPORTANCE OF MY FAITH

My faith is extremely important and defines my life. My faith and family are my rocks. My faith is woven into the fabric of who I am. Whatever gets us through life—the good and the bad—is our go-to, and mine is my unwavering faith in Jesus Christ and the support of my family. I am not perfect in any way, but I know the perfect one, and I have the Bible to go to any time of day or night. I also pray often. I pray for strength, I pray for wisdom, I pray for forgiveness, I pray for patience, I pray for favor, I pray for excellent health for me and my family, I pray for discernment, I pray for healing, and I pray for growth in all aspects of my life. Life is hard to discern, understand, and even live sometimes, and when you have faith, you have strength.

The best prayer you can ever pray for yourself is this: "May the peace of God, which passes all human understanding, keep your heart and mind in the knowledge and love of God." There is nothing like peace, and when you have the peace that surpasses human understanding, you are set. When you have peace, it's like you have a secret, an inner-circle thing, almost like insider trading, that allows you to smile through the pain and live every day with absolute harmony. You realize that sometimes good things fall apart so that better things can fall together. Find your higher power, and you will have peace despite all the issues you face. My higher power is my Lord and Savior, Jesus Christ. I read a lot and have many favorite authors, but my all-time recommended reading material is the Bible. Find your go-to book!

Here are a few of my favorite Bible verses:

- 1 Timothy 6:6—"Godliness with contentment is great gain."
- Philippians 4:6—"Be anxious for nothing, but in everything by prayer and supplication, with thanksgiving, let your requests be made known to God."
- Psalm 23:1—"The Lord is my shepherd, I shall not want."
- Philippians 4:13—"I can do all things through Christ who strengthens me."

It is great to commit a few favorite verses to memory for constant inner strength.

I end this short section with the serenity prayer, which is one of my mom's favorite prayers. Growing up, we had a plaque in the kitchen and another in the living room with those words, and I knew them by heart. However, it wasn't until I was going through my divorce that the words really struck a chord with me. I strive to live my life with "the courage to change the things I can, the serenity to accept the things I cannot, and the wisdom to know the difference."

With strength and peace from above, it is well with my soul and with yours too. Amen.

MY TAKE ON "THE SEVEN HABITS" AND THE DIVORCE PROCESS

As I mentioned earlier, I am a big fan of the Stephen Covey book *The 7 Habits of Highly Effective People* and consider its lessons impactful and tangible. I first read the book in 1996 and then again in the early 2000s, and I am reading it again this year. Each time, I am struck by different aspects of the book, as I am in a different place in life each time. Covey emphasizes that habits require knowledge, skill, and desire, and I completely agree. My trivial four-or-five-cups-a-day-coffee habit is expensive, gives me coffee breath and heartburn, stains my teeth, and gives me palpitations, yet I continue because I have not decided to break that habit. I've had it for so long that it is part of me.

To change unhealthy habits or to create the seven habits of effective people, we need to have the mind-set, support, skills, and will to do so, which is why the book is a must read.

These habits fall into private victories (be proactive, begin with the end in mind, and put first things first), public victories (think win-win, seek first to understand and then to be understood, and synergize), and renewal. If we approach the divorce and postdivorce period thinking of these effective habits, we are more likely to succeed and thrive.

Below are the seven habits and my take on how they apply to us as divorced women and/or moms.

1. **Be proactive:** Once the divorce process starts, be proactive about potential problems and solutions. Do your research, and be prepared. Start exploring avenues to get needed help for the children and for you. Find and engage your support system.
2. **Begin with the end in mind:** Know that the divorce will end, no matter how long and drawn out it is. You want the best outcome for physical, mental, emotional, social, and spiritual health for the children and for yourself.
3. **Put first things first:** Putting the kids first and doing your best to protect them from the collateral damage is the key.
4. **Think win-win:** When you are doing well and the kids are well adjusted, you are in a great place. If the goal is to survive the process and thrive despite the odds, you can approach it by looking for ways to work with your ex to make this happen. It takes a lot to get there—maturity, courageousness, and consideration but, with the support and skills, it can be a priority.
5. **Seek first to understand and then to be understood:** This is the part where you understand where family and friends are coming from and why their reactions to your divorce may not be in sync with yours. You don't have to understand everyone, and you definitely should not try to please everyone, but seek to understand the people you care about.
6. **Synergize:** There is strength in asking for help when needed and accepting help when it is offered. Understand that interdependence is not weakness

and that having a support system and giving back can only make you better.

7. **Renewal:** This is also referred to as "sharpening the saw" by Covey. This is where you replenish your stores and nourish your soul. You celebrate your strengths and victories, big and small. You do this unapologetically, knowing that a happier, rested, refreshed you is a better you for your children and for the world.

In summary, these seven habits take work but can be developed. They can be translated into work, marriage, or other relationships. The first three are private and may not be noticed or celebrated by anyone but you. Once you master those and put them into practice, the next ones will follow and will be public victories as you and the kids thrive. I do hope this short teaser has inspired you to read the Covey book and grow from the lessons offered, as I have.

CHAPTER 2

YOU AND THE CHILDREN

RESOLVE TO PUT THE KIDS FIRST

THIS SEEMS PRETTY obvious, but clearly, it's not so easy in practice. If every divorced couple did this or at least tried to, the kids would likely fare better. It's easier said than done, especially when you are hurt or the divorce is not mutual (it rarely is), but you have to realize that this is not the kids' fault. Regardless of how much you tell them this or reassure them, children often feel guilty about their parents' divorce and blame themselves.

Many psychologists have published on this topic, and this was a recurring theme in the books I read. One of the unintended things you can do is make that guilt worse during the divorce and postdivorce period. *Resolve to put the kids first.* If this is the central thought process for you as a couple going separate ways, it helps. Even if your partner doesn't do this, as the mom, you can drive the process in a positive direction. I know it's hard for some, especially if the divorce occurred because of a huge betrayal and there's another woman or man involved, or your lifestyle or socioeconomic status changes, but you have to do it. Having well-adjusted kids gives you a peace of mind that no protracted, contentious divorce or amount of money can buy. This is not always possible, especially if your ex is abusive, mentally ill, or unstable in any way, but if you are both rational, you can minimize the damage to the kids. Since you can't count on anyone but yourself, plan to be the rational one, and *put the kids first!*

My divorce was not perfect, and I was mad at my co-parent for a long time, but my overarching theme and driving force was putting the kids first. I wanted and needed to beat the odds and get the kids to thrive, not just survive. I told myself that the mad hormones propelled me, thrust me forward, and got things done for us. I know from medicine that statistics are for groups and populations, and you cannot apply statistics to a single patient. These numbers in the published literature guide you, but you have to manage each patient as an individual. I knew the statistics regarding drug use, depression, teen pregnancy, and school-dropout rates did not look great for children of divorce, but I also knew that there were many measured and unmeasured variables that contributed to the final outcome. Those statistics about children of divorce can be attenuated and altered if we, the adults, make the children and their well-being the priority.

I now know that while divorce is not the vision you had for your marriage, your life, or the kids, it can make you a better parent in many circumstances. All the strife, anxiety, insecurity, and worry over keeping the marriage together can distract you from being the parent you want to be. It's hard to see that sometimes, but in my case, I know I am a better parent to my daughters. Many dads will say they feel more useful and hands-on after a divorce. In a married household, dads may be relegated to doing the nonhousehold things, except for taking out the trash or sometimes running errands on the drive home. Let's face it, moms. You think they can't do it right, so you ban them from cooking, helping with homework, or doing the laundry—it's *your* thing. Now when Dad has to host kids, he gets to bond with them over cooking and helping with homework, which is a good thing. The children get the undivided attention of each parent, and you are both more present with them.

When your divorce happens, it can affect your kids in different ways, depending on their ages, genders, and temperaments; how sudden or protracted it was; and how explosive or tense the house was predivorce. Some kids may be relieved, especially if there was a lot of conflict, while others may feel vulnerable, and still others betrayed or abandoned. Regardless of how they feel about the divorce while it's happening, even the kids who are relieved still feel the loss. They need to know that they are heard and loved unconditionally by both parents.

In our case, the divorce was sudden and happened relatively quickly, and the kids and our families felt blindsided. They might also feel helpless, so let them feel like they have some say in their new life. If they have to move houses or schools—and even if they stay in the same home—it's not the same. The kids need consistency, so try to keep some things the same if you can. We had the same nanny for another seven years after the divorce, and that was beyond helpful for me and the children. I realize that in many cases, a single mom may have to move to a different city, and that adds an extra layer of anxiety for the kids. Being able to keep some routines the same and staying in contact with old friends can help provide some stability and constancy for the kids.

Just like you need to go through stages, the kids do also. There are quite a few psychologists who have defined the stages of dealing with loss. There's the Kübler-Ross model, in which the stages include denial, anger, bargaining, depression, and acceptance. There are also the Colin Murray Parkes phases of grief, which include shock and numbness, yearning and searching, disorganization and despair, and finally reorganization. For your children, grief may present as restlessness, poor school performance, getting into fights, hyperactivity or disinterest, poor sleep, clinginess, eating disorders, explosive anger, or despair. Look out for these things, and help them as best you can, using trained professionals as needed.

If you need to let the teachers know what is going on, please do it. Parents are often ashamed or embarrassed to say anything. This can have an effect on the children short term and even long term, as the educators who spend prolonged hours with them may label them as problem children. I know that for some, the cultural issues associated with divorce make it less likely that women will share that information with their children's schools. It's important to realize that the educators are used to dealing with these issues and will maintain confidentiality. This will help the children in the long run. It's really not about you at this point, as you resolve to put the kids first.

To some kids, the divorce does not seem final, and they hold out hope that things will go back to the way they were. A few years ago, mine confessed to me that they always secretly hoped their dad and I would get back together.

Every time we were at a soccer game, band concert, or school event, they hoped we would reunite. The Lindsay Lohan movie *The Parent Trap* was apparently a favorite of theirs, and they actually wanted to plan a similar parent reunion. They were sad on Valentine's Day and when their friends talked about their parents' anniversaries and making gifts. They longed for dinners for four and wanted that perfect family at events, but over time, they accepted the reality of the situation and owned it.

A girl's first love is and should be her father, and for me, it was true. With my father's love, I was able to grow into a confident woman who knew I was loved unconditionally. My first Valentine's Day card was from my dad, who gave all four daughters valentines every year. I remember getting them from the time I was six or seven until I was eighteen. Even now, at forty-six years old, I still get a text or goofy WhatsApp rose with a happy Valentine's Day message from my dad. A father's love and admiration makes a girl confident and allows her to develop a sense of self that will serve her well in life.

I wanted my daughters to have a great relationship with their dad and have the confidence and self-assurance that comes with that. This concept played a significant role in my decision-making process and drove me to put the kids first. We had a joint-parenting agreement, and I never restricted his access to our daughters, even outside the standard agreement. I shared parenting tips with him, and we put on a united front for them at all school and sporting events and every time they needed us.

If you make "Put the kids first" your motto, it drives everything else you do—how you relate to your co-parent, how you speak to your kids about their father, who you expose them to when you are dating, how you listen and speak to them, and how you view yourself. As a mom, the biggest sign of success is not who got to keep the house, how well you made sure they knew Dad dropped the ball, or how much you sacrificed for them. It's raising children who become well-adjusted, compassionate, and confident adults who find their places in the world.

I recently started gardening, and my potted outdoor plants and flowers thrived this spring and summer. I noted a few things that make raising well-adjusted kids similar to growing strong plants:

1. Balance is important. Underwatering or overwatering will cause plants to wilt and die. The same applies to children; we have to love and protect them, but too little affection or drowning them in it can be detrimental to their growth and development.
2. Paying attention is vital. Daily monitoring of weather, shade, and sun conditions can preempt wilting. Be attentive to your kids' verbal and nonverbal cues.
3. Timing is essential. If you notice a waterlogged pot, you can drain it or transfer the plant to another pot. In many cases, this is all you need to do, although sometimes it's too late. Pay attention to big and little things going on in your children's lives and act promptly and accordingly. Even if it looks like the children are too far gone, it's never too late—with nurturing, they will come around.
4. Beautiful, radiant flowers are like well-adjusted kids who thrive despite the odds, and they will always

give you joy, gladden your heart, and bring a smile to your face.

As parents, our goal should be to give our children deep roots so that they are secure, have a sense of self, and know they are loved, and broad wings to fly, grow, and explore the world. We build relationships with them when they are young so that when they leave the home, they chose to remain our friends.

How to put the kids first:

- Resolve to put the children first, and enlist your ex.
- Make it a conscious and deliberate process—write it down if you need to.
- Pray about it, and ask for divine peace and intervention.
- Stay positive, and try to minimize the role of negative, mean-spirited people who want to spur you on in a bloody, drawn-out fight.
- Tell yourself that the kids are innocent casualties of your divorce and should be protected. They did not engage in or provoke the battle.
- Explore why you are so mad and why you want to get back at your ex. Money? The house? Your heart is broken? You want him to suffer? All of the above? Once you figure it out, you will realize that while you may have valid reasons, that battle will harm the kids.
- Reassure the kids, and empathize with them.
- Let the children play active roles in the new home structure. My daughters got to pick paint colors for

their new rooms and had free rein to decorate their walls their way.

- Maintain as much stability from the old home as you can.
- Don't make the children feel like they have to choose sides. They love both parents and should be able to express that guilt-free.
- Treat each child as an individual, knowing that each one may respond in a different way to the divorce.
- Take time to do things with each child separately. While they enjoy family time, they also treasure one-on-one time with you. If they have special interests, make time to do some of those things with them. It makes them feel unique and special. I did Zumba Sundays with Tosin and kickboxing with Funmi. Even if it's not an event, just taking time to get soup together or go for a walk is special.
- Understand that it's never too late to change course and prioritize the kids. Even if you didn't start off that way, kids have an incredible capacity to adapt and, more importantly, forgive.
- Find out how they express their sadness or anger, and encourage them to do so.
- Get professional help for them if they need it, and enlist the school staff as they can often help.

LET YOUR KIDS BE KIDS AND NOT YOUR THERAPISTS

During the divorce process, lots of your emotions and your children's will be on full display. When the kids get angry or sad, complain, whine, or cry, let them be. Don't pump them for details about Dad's dating life or the size of his new place. Don't share every detail of your dating life with them. Don't tell them every detail about why you got divorced or how many child-support payments Dad has missed. Let them be kids.

What if they are sad because he keeps missing his visitation days and never shows up as planned? They have a right to be sad or mad or both, and you can definitely be empathetic. But you can do that without adding your thoughts about what a jerk he is or how all the money is going to his new wife or other negative comments. You may think doing this makes the kids feel better and solidifies the fact that you are the superparent who's always there, but it actually doesn't help things. It may, in fact, backfire. Kids love their parents, and girls especially love their dads. The more you bad-mouth and trash him, the more protective of him they will feel, and they may resent you for it. Sometimes they may lash out and tell you this, but often, they won't because they don't want to hurt your feelings. Sensitive kids who understand your sacrifices may not tell you that they resent what you're doing and that they are now torn, trying to reconcile these statements with the father they love.

If you need to vent about your ex, do it with an adult or a licensed therapist—do not make your kids your therapists. They are dealing with a lot of things already, and they don't need to be your advisers as well.

No divorce is perfect, and no matter how well prepared you are, it can be chaotic and disruptive in small and large ways. Don't trivialize it for the children or others, and acknowledge that it's not the perfect uncoupling. That being said, you have to realize that children and teenagers will be selfish and obnoxious at times, even when their parents are happily married. You can't make everything about the divorce and overindulge the kids. You don't want them to learn to avoid taking responsibility for their actions and to go through life blaming everything on the divorce. Just like I have occasionally pulled the single-mom card to get out of traveling soccer, the girls have pulled the divorce thing to explain away undone homework. You see it, call it out, and *move on.*

Early on, my kids wrote about the divorce, and boy, did they write. My older daughter in particular wrote school essays, poems, conflict papers, innermost thoughts, and journals about our divorce. She even won a poetry/journaling thing by writing about her feelings around it. Writing was her go-to, and she used it all the time. Initially, I wished she didn't, but I soon realized that it made her feel better. For her it was cathartic, and for that I was grateful. It was about her and not me, and that's the way it should be. Fortunately, by the time she was writing her college-application essays, she had written so much about the divorce that it didn't even make her top-five options, and her essay was about her love of music instead. Kids have fewer ways to express their feelings about the divorce, so if they find an outlet, embrace it and hope they don't reveal too many scandalous details at school.

As much as you may want to spend all your time with the kids, it is necessary to separate yourself. It is tempting to spoil them or make them your best friends and have party time all the time, but that is detrimental in the long run. Children need structure, and now more than ever, they need you to be the parent. Adult conversations, events, shows, and situations should remain adult things. Talking to them about the juicy details of your potential online dates or the messy details of your divorce is unhealthy. You may have to pass on a few adult events if you can't get childcare, but it is your role to protect them and let them be kids for as long as they can. Try to protect their innocence.

Having the kids around when you are yakking it up with your BFF or your girlfriends or watching R-rated shows is not good for them. They grow up too fast, and that could harm them in the long run. If you have girls, they might get sassy and talk like you do, which might make other kids uncomfortable. If you have boys, they might feel like the man around the house and think they have to protect you. While this is a noble thing to do, it can be too much too soon. It's forcing them into a role they are not ready for and shouldn't be burdened with.

It's great to be open and honest with children, but it's also fine to compartmentalize and leave some things for the adults in your life. That's why having a group of friends or even one close friend you can share with in a judgment-free zone is helpful.

Sometimes the kids want to know what happened, and moms wonder how much they should share. Sharing when you are still mad or depressingly sad or unaccepting of the divorce is not a good idea and shapes the rest of the process for the kids. Even when all is calm, you don't have to tell them the gory details (if there are any).

Mine were six and seven when we got divorced, didn't ask much, and wouldn't have understood much then. As time went on, they did ask what happened, and my standard refrain remained—"It doesn't matter what happened. What matters is that Dad and I love you unconditionally. Maybe when you're older, we can talk about it more." They have held me to that, and two days before my older daughter left for college, she asked me if I would tell her what happened once she turned eighteen. Really? When I started writing this book, my younger one wanted to know if it was going to be a tell-all book and if she had to wait until I was done to get the juicy details of the divorce. She even had a title for the book—*Exposed!* Really? This is a gentle reminder that kids never forget what you say and will bring your words back verbatim when it's convenient for them.

How to let your kids be kids and not your therapists:

- Maintain the parent-child roles, and don't try to be their best friend. They need and thrive on having you as a parent to provide guidance and structure.
- Share your angst and adult things with other adults—don't dump them on your kids.
- Volunteer together; work out together. This is empowering and is a shared experience that can be therapeutic, but let kids be kids, and you be the adult.
- Let them engage in age-appropriate activities. Some children want to take on adult roles to fill the void, but this is too much too soon.
- Cultivate a judgment-free home where they can express their varied emotions without feeling like they are letting you down.
- Work with a group of trusted people to share child-care duties so you can have adult time.
- Consider family therapy as a way for all to work together with a therapist.

CHAPTER 3

YOU AND YOUR CO-PARENT

MAINTAIN CIVILITY WITH YOUR CO-PARENT

*The single biggest problem in communication is
the illusion that it has taken place.*

—George Bernard Shaw

Maintaining civility is critical. You must do this not
because it's easy, and not because you're a saint, but
because you need to. In any other breakup, people avoid
or limit communication as they get over the relationship. With divorce that is impossible if there are children
involved, and communicate you must. In the beginning,
it is hard! Maybe *brutal* is the way to describe the visceral
reaction I had during any conversation with my ex early
on. We had to talk about the kids, the house, the divorce
agreement, financial stuff, disclosures, vacation time,
time-shares, assets, and so forth. I had to talk about when
and who to tell about the split and how to tell them. The
bottom line is that while your natural instinct is to avoid
this person (which you could do in any other breakup),
because you have kids, *you have to talk.* Talking with my ex
was painful, and the fact that I was mad made it worse.

It's normal to look for ways to get back at the other person, but it's draining and futile, and it ages you. It's so not worth it.

The best invention for—and bonus gift to—divorced parents everywhere is e-mail. Today, it may be WhatsApp or instant messenger, but in 2005, e-mail was king! It's amazing how much better it is to communicate that way until you get to the point that talking is not so disastrous. You are also more productive and can communicate when you want to without being put on the spot. Sure, it wasn't perfect, and I could still use all caps and many exclamation points when I was miffed. I could still use curse words in an e-mail, but it sure beat face-to-face or phone conversations in those first few months to a year. E-mail saved us a lot of angst and got the messages across. Looking back at old e-mails, I sometimes sigh and smile and reflect on how far we've come.

People say time heals all wounds, and just like physical wounds, emotional wounds become less raw over time until they become faint scars. How much you scar and how you look at the scar and remember how you got it depends a lot on your initial reaction to the injury. Initial care and damage control can alter the natural history of the healing. Uncared for and aggravated, the wound can get markedly worse and lead to poor, delayed healing and a horrid outcome with extensive scarring.

Let me give you a relevant example of an infected foot ulcer. In a diabetic, that eventually leads to amputation as the only option to save the host (i.e., the person with the infected foot ulcer). To the outside person, it seems extreme that someone went into the hospital and ended up losing a foot. However, it's lifesaving and necessary. It could have been prevented, but when it reached that point, there was no looking back. And while the person will miss the foot (mourn the loss), he or she looks ahead to living minus the foot, and most important, preventing this unfortunate outcome from happening again. To do this, the person has to embrace the new reality and move forward. Someone who views the amputation as inevitable or just bad luck is unlikely to modify behaviors or be vigilant for early signs, making another amputation likely. This often happens to people with poorly controlled diabetes.

In terms of how this applies to divorce, marriages don't go from perfectly healthy to divorce in an instant. As in the case of the diabetic, there's trauma that leads to the ulcer (bumps and stumbles in the marriage), which, if not cared for, gets infected. There are many options for managing the nonhealing ulcer, including intravenous antibiotics, minor surgical debridements, and revascularization procedures (to divert additional blood supply to the area), all in the hope of delaying or avoiding an amputation. Unfortunately, in some cases, the only long-term, curative, and often lifesaving option is an amputation. The morbidity of a nonhealing infection, the chronic pain, and frequent hospitalizations and procedures can only be alleviated by an amputation in some patients.

This is akin to a divorce after other options to save the marriage have been exhausted. It's important to accept that the divorce is the lowest point, and moving forward to healing is the way to go. Just like the amputee who can't accept the loss of a foot lashes out and can't move forward in a healthy way, so is the divorcée who refuses to accept the divorce and blames herself and the co-parent. Once you accept things, it is easier to remain civil and even friendly with your co-parent.

If you spend the whole time fighting and cursing out your co-parent, the kids won't even have the time or the will to have a relationship with him. In other instances, they may try to protect him from you, defend him unflinchingly, and be blind to any flaws he has. It's like when you tell your daughter she can't date a guy or that you don't like a girl in her group. That is the surest, fastest way to get her to become BFFs with that girl or date the guy. If you're vicious in your attacks on the dad, he becomes a saint who can do no wrong. This backfires on you, with the kids spending every ounce of energy defending him. It's not a healthy relationship, and it's clearly unbalanced. You have to know your triggers and try to avoid them or be proactive about them. You lived with this person and, at one time, loved him dearly, which means you both know the other's triggers and most sensitive areas. (You must admit that it couldn't have been 100 percent bad, right?) When you constantly bash and demean their dad in front of your kids, family, or friends, it makes you look bad, whether you know it or not. If he really was that terrible and you married him, then you were either a poor judge of character or a closet masochist.

If you cannot easily recall any of his good traits or attributes, you may need to write a list and post it on your mirror or on your phone. You can then refer to it anytime you need to remind yourself that your marriage wasn't 100 percent bad. Being civil doesn't mean being passive or being a doormat for the sake of your kids. State what you want, what you will and will not accept, and set limits on your ex's access to you.

Maintaining civility with your co-parent also extends to his spouse if or when he remarries. The earlier you accept that this person is not going anywhere and will be part of your children's lives, the faster you will heal. This person hosts your children when they visit or spend time with their dad, and she should not be demeaned or disrespected by you. If this person treats your children well and doesn't try to take over raising your children, you are lucky, as I was. We are civil, and this has worked out well for my daughters, who spend time with their dad and his family. When you are civil to your co-parent's new spouse, it helps your children overall. They are less angst-ridden when they go over, they feel free to like being there, and they are less anxious about the transitions between the two homes.

I know that at this point, some women reading this book will say, "Of course it's easy for *you* to be civil. You were a two-physician home, with no financial issues or abuse, and his new wife didn't ruin your marriage. It's hardly a sacrifice to co-parent in a civil manner." This is true. I didn't have to move to a different suburb, lose my job, fight for the kids, or suffer financially, so it was easier. However, there were events that made it hard to be civil, and I had to dig deep to come through. For example, it was tough when my co-parent moved back to the neighborhood and to the same school district as our kids with his girlfriend and her daughter, and when he had a new child and I heard about it from the girls while on vacation. Divorce may be easier in certain situations, but it's never easy. Anyone who says divorce is easy has not gone through one.

Be ready for people, including family, friends, or even your ex, to think your civility means you are too soft or—gasp!—you want him back. You cannot live your life being swayed by others, and you need to stay focused and keep your eye on the prize—the well-adjusted kids. Being civil does not mean you are a doormat or lack a backbone; in fact, it is the contrary. It means you are mature and strong enough to put yourself aside for the benefit of your children.

Sometimes it's not your co-parent who does something that makes you get on your knees and pray for strength and patience. Sometimes it's the adorable, clueless darlings you are parenting. My older daughter, being a daddy's girl, often told me she was worried that her dad was working too hard and how much he was on call. This was fine, but sometimes I wanted to yell, "What about me? What am I—your slave?" Or I know you can relate to the scenario when the kids share all the good, bad, and ugly with you and only the good stuff with Dad. You get the school angst, the tears, the frustrations, curfews, and calculus, and Dad gets the awesome report cards and fun times. After years of this, I had to stop, yell, and demand that they please let him in on the bad and ugly preteen and teen angsty stuff too.

More than a decade later, we have remained civil and can actually be in the same room comfortably. We are not best friends, or even close friends, anymore, but at this point, I know we will always look out for each other for the kids' sakes. We text and wish each other happy holidays and birthdays; we are there, united, for major events for the children even though we live in different cities, and we plan vacation schedules for the children. We acknowledge and value our roles in the children's lives, and my co-parent respects my parenting skills and style. Eleven years after our divorce, the joy on our older daughter's face when we drove her to college together, set up her bed and dorm room, and walked around campus with her was indescribable. She needs us and knows that we love her unconditionally. At eighteen, this is a great feeling, and it will make her secure and confident and allow her to thrive away from home.

How to maintain civility with your co-parent:

- Use technology to your advantage: e-mail or text if it's hard to talk without getting angry or sad. This is also a way to review conversations years later and see how you have grown. (Caveat: With emoticons, texts and even e-mails can be as fiery as talking, so try to avoid using emoticons if you can.)
- Communicate the facts, and leave out emotions as much as you can.
- Avoid being obsessed with how quickly he seems to have moved on. This will only make you bitter, not better.
- Try to find the good in your co-parent. This may be difficult, but take it on as a challenge.
- Set limits on his access to you, and be clear about what you will and will not accept.
- Try not to compare yourself to his new girlfriend or wife. If she is younger than you, that can make you feel bad, and if she is older than you, it will make you feel worse.
- Do not spend a lot of time imagining what life would have been. If you dwell on the bigger house you gave up, it's hard to be civil to your ex. Instead of living

in the past, live in the present, and embrace the life you have.

- Do not blame your ex for your unhappiness, and realize that happy couples are not divorced.
- Share parenting tips you find helpful. I did this, and my co-parent was receptive.
- Remember, it is all about the kids.
- Pray and meditate.

IT IS NOT A COMPETITION

You have to keep telling yourself that it's not a competition. Some people are naturally competitive (me), and divorce brings it out in others. Something about the divorce process can bring out the competitive, sometimes ugly edge. Many exes compete for the children's affection or attention; for the bigger home; or to be the first to date, the first to remarry, and even the first to move on. The best a kid can have is a balanced and loving relationship with both parents if both parents are able and willing to be in his or her life.

Do not advocate for sole custody or plan to do it all alone just to get the trophy for being the best parent. If you are the residential parent, which many women are, it's not unusual to feel like you are there just for the basics—the mundane, hard parts of parenting—and the other parent gets to be the cool, fun one who sees the kids when everything is fabulous. Let's face it: you do the unglamorous tasks—nightly homework, sick days, angst about last-minute projects and school social issues—and you have to play bad cop, whereas Dad gets to do vacations and gifts. Gifts are always a way to woo kids, and many nonresidential parents, especially dads, can go overboard with them. It may be a way to let the kids know he still cares or to assuage guilt, especially if you are supermom. If you think about it, the nonresidential parent is probably anxious or nervous having the children, and new toys, trips, and gadgets are welcome distractions or ice breakers.

Remember, it's not a competition. You are doing what's important—caring for and raising the kids—and your role is not one that can be quantified in money or gifts. That said, it's tempting to want to compete with gifts of your own. Sometimes, moms will buy things they cannot afford just to match or one-up a co-parent. This is not a wise thing or a good use of resources (college tuition, anyone?), especially if you end up spoiling the kids. Anyone who has raised or been around kids knows that the attention span devoted to a new toy or gadget has a direct correlation to their ages, and it's all measured in minutes. Also, if the kids key into this competition, they may start to play you against each other in a way that heightens the gift giving.

If the gifts are frequent or too expensive, have a discussion with your co-parent. Make sure to do this in a calm, rational manner, and approach it from a good place rather than a vindictive one. This can be in person, on the phone, or through text or e-mail, depending on where you are in your relationship as divorced co-parents.

I remember when I had that discussion with my co-parent. It was two years into our divorce, and after yet another set of expensive just-because gifts for my under-nines, we had to have the talk. I didn't want spoiled, entitled brats who had absolutely no wants and got expensive, over-the-top gifts every week. Our talk was by e-mail and went well. We decided that if we wanted to buy anything that cost more than $150 for the girls other than for birthdays or Christmas, we had to run it by the other parent. This slowed things down a lot, and the excessive gift giving was down to a minimum. Communication is the key and a win-win for the kids and the wallet.

I was financially secure and could have tried to match or outdo him, but that would not have been healthy for our kids or for their college plans. We had set up college plans for them much earlier, and we both agreed that in the long term, funding those was a much better way to show our love and assuage our guilt about the divorce.

There are many ways you can undermine all your hard-earned progress if you stay in competition mode. In addition to the unnecessary energy depletion, it can be financially deleterious. No matter how much money you make or how well-off you are postdivorce, you and your ex are maintaining two households, and things change more for some than others. Be honest with yourself about what you can and cannot afford, and don't try to outdo your co-parent.

How to avoid competing with your ex:

- Remind yourself often that it's not a competition.
- Remember that the best things in life are free and no gifts can ever replace the love of a mother.
- Set limits for gift giving, and discuss with your co-parent. This can be a difficult one, so use e-mail or text if you can't have a civil conversation.

- Do not allow others to get you off track, and don't compare yourself to others.
- Understand that the children see and appreciate all the unglamorous things you do even if they don't squeal with delight every night you check their homework.
- Remind yourself that you don't want overindulged, spoiled kids.

CHAPTER 4

YOU, THE DIVORCE, AND OTHERS

DO YOUR RESEARCH

To BE BETTER prepared for the process and the world around you during and postdivorce, you need to do your research on everything. This can be thought of as gathering intel and evaluating recommendations. Do your research before picking your lawyer, mediator, real-estate agent, therapist, or anything major related to your divorce. This is a big one, and for someone like me, it was crucial. I am a physician-researcher and love to read and explore. The majority of things we do in medicine are evidence based, and I am used to looking up evidence to support my decisions.

The evidence I had before my divorce was that kids of divorce were statistically more likely to have psychological issues, abuse drugs, get pregnant as teenagers, engage in high-risk behaviors, have relationship issues, and the list goes on. That was what I was determined *not* to have happen to my darlings. I needed to know exactly what the odds were, who was studied, what subsets had the lowest risk, and how to make sure the odds were in my children's favor. I knew I couldn't apply statistics to a single individual and that every case was unique. Those statistics highlighted important issues to be aware of, but they certainly didn't mean that these issues affect every child of divorce. I was determined that my girls would be exceptions to these depressing statistics, God being my help.

Now here is where my being a nerd really helped. I know how to research and navigate the literature, and wow, there was a lot out there on divorce. Many books were written by psychologists, relationship experts, lawyers, and researchers and were technical, but some were easy to read and practical. This was a decade ago. And while today, people can turn to blogs, websites, and apps for information, I went about it the old-fashioned way and read a lot of books. I also read books to my girls and made them read simple, illustrated books on divorce. I even made my co-parent read pertinent chapters so we could do the right thing. I still remember sending books over in the girls' backpacks with pages tagged for their dad to read.

I had to read because I had no personal references to guide me through the process. My amazing parents and siblings, whom I trust with my life, were all happily married or still single at the time. None of my high-school or college friends were divorced either. I only knew of one person at work who was going through a divorce, and while we weren't close initially, the process bonded us. I knew that divorces were not uncommon (50 percent stats out there), but in my world, I was the exception. My colleagues had all been married for years, and all my mom friends in my close-knit community were married. There were a few single moms, but they were more casual acquaintances than friends. So I read a lot, and a decade later, I'm still reading.

To see how the data regarding children of divorce were obtained and how to improve the odds for my children, I searched the literature like I would for medical decisions. In medicine, we have different levels of recommendations for rating the evidence that supports our clinical decisions. They go from level one to level four. Level one refers to randomized clinical trials, level two refers to large observational studies, level three refers to case series, and level four refers to expert opinion. In any studies, conclusions reached with level-one evidence would be the strongest.

Level 1
This level consists of looking at two different strategies, and then following kids over time to see outcomes after controlling for things like gender, age, parents' ages, income, duration of marriage, civil or hostile divorce, socioeconomics, personality type, and so on. But how do you control for all these variables? How do you measure outcome? How do you define success? As you can see, this cannot be done, and the evidence is not there.

Level 2
This is an observational study of a large group of kids over time to see what practices were different between well-adjusted kids and those who were not. Some of these observations are available and are useful but have limitations. These limitations are those unmeasured or uncontrolled factors that drive the differences in outcomes.

Level 3
This would involve observing small groups of kids and different practices to see commonalities and trends. These are more common than the previous two and provide some insight.

These are studies that tell us that when we strive to put the kids first and minimize conflict, the children do better.

Level 4
On this level, a group of people make recommendations based on their experiences to formulate an expert opinion. This is the weakest level of recommendation and in medicine is a last resort. We use these only when we have nothing else (such as with a new or rare condition), and we use them fully aware of their flaws, biases, and potential failure. It's the "at least we have something/what is there to lose?" level of recommendation.

Now that you know how we rate recommendations, it's pretty clear that expert advice is only as good as the expert. A lot of information is written about divorce by experts, but because there are so many unmeasured variables, we cannot generalize all the conclusions to all children of divorce. What is clear is that positive parenting and resolving to put the interests of the kids first is always a good thing. Speaking of experts, we all know people who consider themselves experts on all topics (they are not), have advice because they know someone who was divorced (biases abound), are older than you and want the best for you, or just want to talk and share horror stories with you (misery loves company). These are *not* helpful, can drain you of all energy and resolve, and can undermine your intentions to put the kids first.

I avoided and rejected unsolicited advice and found good books. I found that while the odds for bad outcomes among divorced kids are high, they are not absolute. I found books on how to minimize those risks, I found books for children, I found books on stages of divorce, and I found a few self-help books about being a single mom. If you don't like to read, listen to audiobooks. The Internet is an excellent resource, but you can get lost and distracted from your mission. There are blogs, but just like ratings for movies and services, they can bring out extreme opinions. For some reason, those with horrid, negative experiences are more vocal, devote more time to sharing their views, and may dominate the group chats. Again, it's hard to rate the evidence, and you may be listening to a bunch of supposed experts with axes to grind.

If you think about it, we research almost everything we do. So why wouldn't you do it for this big decision with important ramifications? We research restaurants, big-ticket purchases, vacation destinations, childcare, preschools, tutors, and the list goes on. You wouldn't let a surgeon operate without doing some research first. So, while word of mouth and personal opinions may be freely offered, go to the source, and rank the evidence before committing. Think about this as you make decisions for yourself and your children during the divorce and in the years that follow.

How to do the research:

- Go to the library or search online for good books on divorce and co-parenting. You are reading this book, so you are already ahead of the pack.
- Share good tips that you find with your co-parent, and apply those tips in situations that come up.
- Use your best learning method, whether that's visual; audio; short bursts; or long, slow processing. Do you!

- Limit and vet the advice you get, both solicited and unsolicited. Like my dad says, when you get advice, there are only three things you can do: (1) accept, (2) reject, or (3) accept with modifications. Know your sources, their intentions and motives, and where they are coming from, and then decide what the information you are getting means. Remember, misery loves company, and many people consider themselves content experts.
- Seek out and talk to other single moms whom you admire or respect.
- Research professionals in related fields: lawyers, psychologists, counselors, and mediators, and use their services.

YOUR DIVORCE WILL SCARE PEOPLE

This is fascinating and sometimes hurtful. It's like divorce makes the people around you weird and unhinged. They can get anxious or overly critical. The isolation from some, the knowing looks from others, the pitiful stares, the gossipy innuendos, the slow withdrawals, and the decrease in party invitations may be sudden, as though divorce were a highly contagious infection. In some cultures, the parents of the divorced woman become social outcasts, which may affect the marriageability (not a commonly used word, I know) of the other siblings. It's like divorce is a genetic defect that could be transmitted in the bloodlines. A divorced woman may affect how her whole family is perceived. Even though it takes two to tango and uncouple, the failure of a marriage can fall squarely on the woman. In my culture, phrases like *too proud, too independent, too educated, feminist,* and *too Americanized* are thrown around to explain why she didn't fight for her marriage. In some cases, even the children are treated as pariahs.

Why would people do this? Sometimes it's because they are scared. The more perfect your marriage seemed, the more scared and uneasy they are when it ends. I found out that what scares us the most are the things that could happened to us at any time. Yes, people are scared of heights, spiders, snakes, zombies, and flying, but you can avoid these things if you choose and be just fine. Things like sudden illness, a car crash that leaves you disabled, a child with a drug problem, and divorce scare the hell out of us. These are real, "could happen no matter what you do" things and seem to happen to people just like us. Your picture-perfect life could be sailing along, and then boom! One (or all) of these things happens to you.

To cope with the unease or anxiety surrounding issues like divorce, people move away from it, ostracize the people involved, or talk about it. It's as though they think that if the divorced mom and kids don't come by their houses anymore, they'll be spared the divorce curse (ha ha). It forces some to evaluate their own marriages and confront the possibility of a life postdivorce. Many don't mean to hurt you, but they don't know what to say or how to say it and would rather avoid you altogether. Others, who were friends of the couple, would rather not take sides and just give you the slow fade. Having your children around may lead to questions from theirs, such as, Why doesn't your ex live in the house? Why do your kids get two Christmas celebrations? Or will their parents get a divorce too?

Once you know why people react this way, you don't take it personally. I'm not saying it doesn't hurt to lose friends (they really weren't friends), but it's not personal. It's a self-preservation thing for them. Take time to reflect on what you thought when you saw single moms before your divorce. Did you judge them? Shy away from them? Another issue is the myth of the thirsty divorcée. This is the irrational notion that you, as a single mom, will pounce on and take any man, including the overweight husband of your friend/acquaintance/colleague/neighbor. Yuck! If you are good looking and confident around men, that means you want them even more. This makes some women uncomfortable to have you around their men. There are also some married men who think you are easy prey and theirs for the picking if you come over to hang with their wives or chaperone playdates. I have heard a few tales of propositions that would make your skin crawl. These creepy males need to be checked, and I'm sure that many of you have had to do so during your postdivorce journey. While there probably are some divorced women who cannot find a man even with the countless amazing apps and sites out there and only want a married man, I can safely say they are the tiniest minority. The vast majority of us have too much going on and are not looking at someone else's man. *We definitely do not want him.* For me, this was a real problem, and to avoid any perceived I'm-stealing-your-man moves, I socially isolated myself from many couples. For years I have mainly socialized with close friends, amazing women, and my siblings. It's safer, and for me, it's the best decision.

If you do socialize broadly, be aware of these issues—real and perceived—and set boundaries. If you sense that a woman is uncomfortable having you around her man or a married man is giving you unwanted attention, remove yourself from those situations. We are women, and our intuition is God given for a reason, so listen to it. Don't use the unwanted attention to make yourself feel better or to get back at your ex or to spite a friend who shunned you during your divorce. Do not be that spiteful woman who wants everyone else to get divorced and makes everyone uncomfortable with words and innuendos. These are not healthy behaviors and will only perpetuate the ugly myth of the desperado divorcée. Let's break that cycle.

In closing, I would like to emphasize that I have tons of married friends, and most couples will remain your friends and behave in a civil, respectable, nonjudgmental manner toward you and your children. The examples above illustrate the few who do not, and thankfully, they are in the minority.

How to cope with reactions to your divorce:

- Understand why your social relationships may change, and don't take it personally.
- Talk to your children if they get excluded, and find ways to make new friends together.
- Don't put yourself in situations where your friends or their husbands perceive you as a thirsty divorcée.
- Learn to do things yourself or pay for the service. Don't have your friend's boyfriend or husband help you move, change porch lights, build a porch, or hang up Christmas lights. There are lots of services and handy apps to use.

- Call out bad behavior when you see it, and don't accept nonsense from anyone.
- Don't become bitter or spiteful. You don't want to be *that* woman.
- Appreciate old friends who stick with you, don't pity you, and just let you be.
- Be open to new friends, both married and single. You will be amazed by how much you can learn about yourself.

UNDERSTAND THAT IT'S HARD FOR YOUR EXTENDED FAMILY AND CLOSE FRIENDS

If divorce is uncommon or frowned upon culturally, or if your family loved your spouse like mine did, they may pray, and try for a while, to get you back together. It's annoying and exasperating when you know it's not going to happen, but understand that they are just hoping. Just like the children who wish and hope and pray that Mom and Dad will get back together, the parents are doing that too. That annoyed me and sometimes made me hostile toward my parents, as I couldn't understand why they couldn't accept things and move on. They hoped for years and sometimes told me stories of couples who separated for prolonged periods and then got back together. These stories made me laugh out loud or shudder in horror, and I often asked them to stop. I found myself reminding them often that I was divorced not separated.

Eventually, I realized that I had to be patient with them and understand that they were never privy to the issues going on in my marriage. To them, we seemed perfect together, and that made it hard for them to move on. They had been married for more than three decades and felt we didn't fight hard enough to keep the marriage. They felt that being in America made it easy for us to walk away from the marriage. They also felt helpless, thinking that if they had known we had issues early on, they could have helped. They knew that in our Nigerian culture, like many others, the woman is blamed for the divorce, and they wanted to protect me from any gossip or ill thoughts. They were doing what parents do by trying to put me first. They also wanted the best for their grandkids, which, in their experience, meant a stable home with two parents. Once I realized where they were coming from, I was able to go easy on them and let them take the time to process the divorce, mourn the loss of the marriage, and absolve themselves of any guilt. Then they were able to join me in the process of moving on.

My parents are amazing people who pray for each of their children, in-laws, and grandchildren by name daily and have always prayed for my co-parent. They pray for his health, success, and happiness and wish him well. They know that he loves his kids and that his being there for them makes them happy and confident. They are my role models, and I adore them. My siblings, being of a different generation, were able to accept the divorce earlier and move on with me. Their unwavering support in a myriad of ways has kept our trio going.

For some of our Nigerian friends (few, not all), some of the same issues came into play. Since most people stayed married to the end (sometimes the bitter, dysfunctional end), our getting divorced in our thirties was a no-no. They couldn't understand it, and I faced a varied set of reactions ranging from curiosity to criticism. The most common I heard was that the American/Western culture of easy divorce was to blame. People said things like, "This America makes people move on too fast," "People don't fight for marriages in America," "Divorce is so easy in America," "You people—America has made you liberated," and, "There are too many options and choices in America." Or the narrative was about me as a woman in America, forgetting how men are and being too American. Since no one knew the details of my divorce, people offered their two cents: Are you divorcing because he cheated? What did you do? Did he want a son? How about trying for a son?

What all this meant was that, all things being equal, we wouldn't have been divorced if we lived in Nigeria. There, we look away from transgressions, and divorced women are scorned by society. That way of thinking places the reasons for divorce onto the American culture and not the two people in the marriage. This is not ideal or true, but as we know from Civics 101, socially accepted norms affect our decisions profoundly. If divorce is not accepted by society or divorcées are treated like pariahs, we stay no matter how dysfunctional things are because it's what we do. In some cultures, having a cheating spouse, one who abandoned the family, an abusive (physically or emotionally) spouse, or one who is emotionally checked out, may be better than being single.

Some people who criticize you are curious and wonder what it feels like to be single again. When people ask me if I'm lonely, I explain that I may be alone, but I am not lonely. I also state that marriage does not provide immunity against loneliness. And really, I am not alone—I have my children, family, and friends who care about and adore me.

When divorce happens, the two people involved have lost something. It is never easy, wherever you live or whatever your culture. You are less likely to be ostracized or openly blamed in America, but the issues and hurt remain the same. As the years have gone by, I have met amazing Nigerian women in America who are new single moms, separated, or divorced, and I've found that we face similar issues and challenges no matter how things happened. We all want the best for our kids, are straddling two different cultures, want to be happy, and are anxious about this phase and the future. It's not easy, but we make it work, and these women are raising amazing children while being boss ladies at work. Again, as you get unsolicited feedback from people after your divorce, remember how they were socialized and where they are coming from. Everyone looks at situations through their own lenses, and perceptions often differ.

What can you do about how the divorce affects others?

- Give them time to go through the phases of loss too. You've had more time to prepare.
- Realize that they are not privy to the inner workings of the marriage, and to them, all seemed perfect.
- Understand where they are coming from and their cultural influences.
- Let them know that you are doing well. The best way for them to move on is if they see you doing well.

- Let them know how they can help, if they seem genuine, so that they feel useful.
- Avoid negativity and negative people who drain your energy.

SHARE SPARINGLY: WHY IS EVERYONE SO OBSESSED WITH MY DIVORCE?

No matter how much you want to vent and complain or let others know how much you were hurt, you need to keep some things to yourself. For a myriad of reasons, this one is important. Details about your marriage and its ending should be kept to a minimum. Don't share everything with everyone; instead, do a lot of listening, nodding, and smiling. You will run into many people who seem overly curious or concerned, and with the divorce rate at approximately 50 percent, you may wonder why this topic still evokes so much angst and curiosity. In addition to the close family and friends who genuinely care, you have neighbors, friends, gym and yoga friends, work friends, and colleagues all wanting to know details. Some people want to see the inner workings of how a married couple becomes a divorced couple. It's a way to compare their marriages to yours without saying that overtly, a way to understand how this divorce thing happens. Those intrusive questions may be a way for others to do diagnostics on their own marriages and predict if divorce is in their future. For some it's plain curiosity, while, for others, it's a juicy distraction from the goings-on in their lives.

Some people are subtle; some are less subtle. I had people ask me if it was infidelity. Did he cheat? Did I cheat? Was it a financial thing? Gambling? Who asked for the divorce? How much were our assets? How long was the process? Was the sex bad? *Really?* How brazen, but oh well.

You can't stop people from being nosy or intrusive, but you can control what you share. It's your life, your marriage, and no one else's business. Perfect marriages don't end in divorce, and although some people think it's better to stay in a failing marriage, once you are divorced, you need to keep looking ahead and moving forward. Sometimes it's a clear case of misery craving company. A few people may think you're taking the easy way out and not fighting to make things work. Anyone who thinks that divorce is the easy way out has not had to go through one. The final results and life postdivorce may be the best things that could have happened, but the process is never easy.

When people ask you questions about your divorce, the way that you respond and the emotion in your words and actions really affect how those conversations proceed. Don't feel obliged to share your personal information with others. Word gets around, and sometimes it gets back to your children, family, coworkers, or even your co-parent, which can damage the co-parenting process or ruin your standing in the community.

How to share sparingly (if at all):

- Have a full and interesting life. If you have a lot going on, talking about your divorce doesn't even make the cut in any conversation.
- Know situations when you are prone to spilling your guts and avoid being around others then (e.g., after

you have been drinking, right after drop-off, or when the children are being extra feisty).

- Identify nosy or intrusive people and try to avoid them or have a ready answer with a smile, such as "I'm fine, thanks, but I'd rather not talk about the divorce."
- Ask, "How's your marriage going?" if the nosy or intrusive people remain persistent after your ready answer.
- Figure out ways to change the narrative, and highlight the positive things and growth you are experiencing postdivorce.

HELP ME!

Asking for or accepting help when it is offered is *not* a sign of weakness. Knowing when you need help and where and who to ask for help is a sign of maturity and confidence. Pride can be an issue, as it is for me sometimes. We are proud of being strong women, and it remains essential that we know and acknowledge this daily; however, asking for help does not diminish this in any way. You cannot do it all, and sometimes you need help. It could be someone to help with the school run or picking up from soccer practice, an afterschool sitter, or sharing grocery runs. There are other women in your community who are willing and want to help you. You just need to ask, or at least say yes when they offer.

I have been fortunate to live in Oak Park, Illinois, for the last twenty-three years, and I cannot imagine a better place to live, raise children, or be a mom, especially a single mom. The people are amazing, and we will always remember our time here fondly. The women and couples I have met and become friends with have always been there for us. I have been part of book clubs, mom-daughter book clubs, bunco groups, and moms'-night-out groups. I have had friends to take dance and language classes, attend fundraisers, watch playoff games, and go to art events with. My community has offered to pick up my kids from practice when I am running late; drop my kids at school on snowy, freezing days when I am at work already; pick up the schedule for prep classes; and just help make my life easier in ways big and small. It took me a while to get there, because in the early years I wanted to prove to myself and to everyone else that I was so awesome that I could do everything by myself. It's easy to wear your independence and strength as a badge of honor and to default to the supermom complex. It may feel empowering for a while, but it gets tiring. You may also wind up alienating people who would otherwise like to help.

Remember, too, that your community does not only mean where you live. You may find that your community is at work, church, or the gym. If someone offers help and the offer seems genuine, please accept it. Occasionally, help comes from unexpected sources, and new alliances and friendships are formed. Be open to help when offered.

An analogy to knowing when to ask for or accept help is what happens in health care with our trainees. In the hospital, there are students, interns, residents, fellows, attendings, and senior attendings, all with different levels of training and a vast range of experience. The medical student who graduates after years of schooling is suddenly thrust into caring for patients as a doctor. While the interns and residents stay the long overnight hours and see patients, there is always on-site supervision. There are senior residents and fellows in house, and attendings are on call or on-site, or only a page or phone call away. While there are scheduled supervision, sign outs, huddles, and run-throughs in which patients are discussed, there is also a level of autonomy. This means that the interns and junior residents have the first contact with new patients overnight, are usually running around putting out fires, are often tired and bleary-eyed (sound familiar?), and have to make important decisions. A sign of maturity and growth is knowing when to call for backup, page the senior, or call the attending. You don't want to be the overconfident, cocky intern who doesn't call for backup when you should or the overly pleasant but clearly exhausted one who just wants to be a martyr. Both situations are prone to causing errors, and the outcomes could be horrid. This may seem extreme, but it's really not.

The martyr attitude may lead to burnout and alienation of others. Interns may ask for help more often initially, but as they learn more and become more comfortable, they will call for backup less but will recognize situations in which they need it. Backup is not always the senior doctor. Often, an astute resident knows and values the importance of teamwork and uses all the resources at his or her disposal. The entire health-care team, with varied expertise and different levels of experience, is there to achieve the best patient outcomes. Any physician who does not understand this and tries to go it alone will burn out quickly; alienate many; and, in the worst-case scenario, will have poorer patient outcomes. Excellent physicians value the team, accept the help of others, and appreciate the synergy of a well-oiled team. Use your network, and tap into the resources you have available to you.

The savior complex is real, and sometimes people thrive on your despair. So if it seems like the stronger you get, the fewer calls or texts you get from certain friends, that's OK. Don't take it personally. Those people were in your life for a reason or season, and when their work was done, they moved on to the next person who needed saving.

When you seek out or accept offered help, it doesn't make you weak or pathetic. It means you are strong enough to know your strengths and your weaknesses. Like the intern running around every fourth night in the hospital, ask for help when you need it and accept help when it's offered. Know that this will lead to better outcomes for you and your children. Being the supermom martyr can deplete your stores and could eventually affect your ability to be the best mom and woman you can be.

How to ask for and accept help:

- Be open—not needy, clingy, or helpless, just open.
- Understand and harness the power of your network.
- Know your limitations, and accept them as limitations, not weaknesses. I realized I wasn't good with crafts, baking, or calculus, so I tapped into my network or outsourced.
- Realize that your biggest competition is yourself, so take care of yourself.
- Know that this is not about you; it's about the kids. You need to recharge, and asking for help allows you to be a better mom for them.

- Exchange services with other moms in your network, such as childcare, hair braiding, and soccer drop-offs.
- Join an online community where you can share and exchange ideas and services.
- Remember to pay it forward.

EMBRACE AND SUPPORT OTHER SINGLE MOMS

Don't buy into that bullshit about the hierarchy of single moms. You don't know what I'm talking about? Yes, you do! The dumb hierarchy that society likes to place on single moms only divides us. Let's be honest—we have all had weird thoughts or misconceptions about single moms at some point (myself included), and this only tears us apart. Here is society's way of defining single moms:

- Widowed single mom (something bad happened to you)
- Divorced single mom (you had everything right, and then you did something wrong and lost it all)
- Single mom by choice (you had your career and then decided late to just go it alone)
- Young or teen single mom (you didn't plan to have kids and are struggling because you made bad choices)

While single moms may differ in age, socioeconomics, race, and occupation, what unites us is that we are women raising children. In all these cases, except for the widowed mom, the co-parent may or may not be in the picture, and this can add a level of complexity.

As a young-looking woman, I have met people who look at me with my girls in a condescending manner or tell me, "You must have had them really young." When they found out I was a divorced physician who had my kids when I was twenty-eight and twenty-nine, they suddenly wanted to become my friend or have the girls over for a playdate. This should not be the case, but sadly, it is. As women, we should *not* do this to one another. Regardless of how we became single moms, we all have the same goal—to raise successful, well-adjusted children. Once we realize this, we can stick up for one another, stand with one another, and support one another. Support each other in the workplace, at social events, and on the sometimes-vicious school playgrounds, where the cliques can be devastating.

Maya Angelou once said, "I've learned that people will forget what you said, people will forget what you did, but people will never forget how you made them feel." This is a profound truth because our nonverbal cues and messages resonate with people, including the kids. No matter how dire your circumstances may be, know that you can make your children feel loved and nurtured.

This also extends to how we relate to other moms, single or not. Sometimes children have moved a lot so their moms can find jobs or better opportunities, and it's already difficult for them to settle in and make friends. When we as the adults ostracize their moms, treat them in a shoddy manner, or exclude them from playdates, we are inadvertently adding to their hurt.

Sometimes it's hard to make ends meet, and single moms may feel like they are not doing enough for the kids. The neighbors may seem to always be on vacations or have private lessons and tutors, all of which may make you feel insecure. There are ways to expose your kids to culture and events without breaking the bank, and it's important to know that children will always value quality time spent with parents who love them. Kids remember experiences and time spent with you and will adjust to any lifestyle if you seem OK with it. They are looking to us for cues, and if we are good, they are good.

How can we support one another?

- Realize there is a kinship created in shared experiences. That bond of raising children outside the traditional family setting and wanting the best possible outcomes for our children unites us. Examples are team athletes and soldiers, who often bond for a lifetime because of events, experiences, or difficulties they share.
- Don't judge or compare how you became single moms. This is not helpful and can be hurtful. Judging or comparing makes you bitter and can hurt another mom.
- Acknowledge that we are all different, have different experiences, and want different things for our lives. Don't try to make your opinions someone else's facts. I wasn't interested in dating, being coupled up, or being a wife again, but I have never knocked someone else for wanting these things and will always support my friends.
- Advocate for one another, and try to make things easier for other moms. When my children were

younger, the elementary school had PTO meetings and volunteer opportunities only at certain times. Realizing that single moms may have issues with childcare or leaving work, we knew that we needed to advocate for morning and evening meetings and that childcare was available at evening meetings to ensure full participation. Single moms care about their kids' education but may not have the flexibility or resources to be at all meetings.

- Share resources with other moms, such as tutoring resources, summer camps, scholarship opportunities, and so on.
- Consider sharing childcare responsibilities on certain weekends so moms can go out to get their party on or stay home to relax kid-free for a few hours.
- Public libraries and museums are gold mines and treasure troves of information for children.
- Make friends with your school counselor, especially once your kids get to middle school and, more importantly, high school.
- Talk to the room parent or that mom who has all the information. They are usually willing to share information, so don't be shy.

CHAPTER 5

YOU AS YOU GROW

HAVE A SUPPORT SYSTEM

HAVING A SUPPORT system is an essential component in your divorce-transition tool kit; it cannot be overstated. Every woman needs a support system, but it's especially crucial if you are a single mom. Your support crew is there to make you the best person and help you be the best mom you can be. Remember, it's all about putting the kids first.

In medicine, it's about putting the patient first. Lead physicians understand that while the buck stops with them, the entire health-care team is critical to an excellent outcome. Just like you cannot pour from an empty jar, a depleted mom cannot provide optimal care. A depleted physician is no good to anyone and can actually be detrimental. Your support system comes from a variety of places, some of which are obvious (family, close friends) and some of which are new and pop up unexpectedly (your nanny, an old high-school friend, your yoga instructor, a work colleague).

My main support system is my family. They have been a constant source of love, support, and encouragement for me and the girls. They are there in ways I cannot describe, and having that wall to protect us and a safety net to catch us has made this journey one of personal growth and tremendous appreciation for family. I have been blessed with parents who were college sweethearts and are still married forty-seven years later. The times we've spent with my parents have helped my children blossom and grow and see what the love of parents looks like even when you're in your forties. They pray for the kids and grandkids daily and have made our happiness their life projects.

My siblings are my go-to peeps and embody all the things anyone could need and want. They are all gorgeous and handsome (bro) and have provided constant love and support to the kids and me. They have different personalities, strengths, and weaknesses, and they bring so much into our lives by being who they are. We have go-to aunts and an uncle (shout-outs to TC, AO, EO, and IF) to help with college essays and interviews, travel with, joke with, talk to at night, strategize with, and bond with at any time of day or night. They are always one phone call, text, e-mail, FaceTime, or WhatsApp away and have made it easier to raise these wonderful girls.

I do realize not everyone is blessed with this type of family, but it is unreal how many times a divorce may help heal damaged family relationships and make these relationships stronger. I have seen estranged family members put aside differences, rally around a newly separated parent, and become pillars of support. Sometimes old friends become closer, or a new friend emerges and becomes a close friend for this next phase in life—KR, you rock! My friend KR took me to Mexico on the first anniversary of my divorce, and it was great to be away that first year. To celebrate the anniversary of my divorce for the first few years, I tried to do something fun that day. Eventually, with the demands of life, I actually forgot the date, and now I can't remember the last time I did something special to celebrate that day.

Instead, I celebrate each day and am thankful for all that I have and the woman that I am.

I have a few friends, both old and new, who have become sisters to me and second moms to the kids. They are women who have grown with us and shared so much love with us. This support system is important and necessary to help you grow and be the best you.

The support is there for you and for the kids. A rested mom is a happy mom, and when Mom is happy, everyone is happy. This support may vary, as you need different things depending on what stage of life you are in, how old the kids are, how your finances are doing, and how involved your ex is in co-parenting the children. If you work outside the home and can afford it, please get a nanny or consistent childcare provider. It costs money but will give you peace of mind and provide some consistency for the kids, especially if you hit the jackpot. Stella came into our lives when my younger daughter turned three and is still my call-in-a-pinch person fourteen years later. She worked with us full time even after the girls started school, and though her role has changed over the years, the one constant was that she was there to care for my kids. She loves them unconditionally and continues to play a big role in their lives. Her Valentine's Day, Easter, Christmas, and birthday cards for us are the first to arrive, and she checks in with us all the time. My older daughter is in college and calls her periodically just to chat. When I got divorced, sold my house, and bought a new home, she was a constant during the changing times.

Support can also come from coworkers, neighbors, or a school playground group that meets a need at that stage. A support system may be readymade and fall into place, but sometimes you need to seek it out. It's important to remain perceptive and understand that you need to set and keep boundaries with your support system. Being there for you does not mean people get unlimited, unfettered access to you and your family. You should also give back and pay it forward. Other newly divorced women may look to you for support as they go through the early stages, and if you have healed or at least moved on from the raw, harsh initial stages, be willing to support them.

Consider joining a support group if you think it might make you feel better to be around other people who are going through the same situation. Hearing other people in similar situations share their struggles, having others hear your struggles, and getting support from people who know your struggles can help strengthen you. This is certainly not for everyone, and it was not for me. I was more of a deal-with-it-yourself, private person, and I recharged and drew energy from periods of stillness and solitude. Support groups often meet in person somewhere in your community, such as a church, but increasingly, they can be found online. Do the research, and find what works for you. Sometimes, the well-meaning friends and family you have cannot meet that need because they are not in your situation, and a support group fills that need. Only you will know how much to engage and when it's time to disengage. You may find that, on a personal level, you are ready to leave the support group, but you stay to encourage others who are starting off where you were a few weeks, months, or years ago. This is the part where you give back, which is part of the personal-growth phase.

A therapist can play a key role in this process, and for many people it is necessary, even lifesaving. I finally went to see a therapist a year after my divorce. It wasn't because something had happened; it was what had *not* happened. I felt like I wasn't sad enough—I never hit that can't-function crippling state. I was going and going, and I was worried that I would one day suddenly lose it in a destructive manner. I even jokingly gave my division chair a heads-up, telling him that if he ever got the call from the ward that his star faculty was rolling around on the floor or yelling like a maniac and punching people in the face, he should blame it on my divorce. He laughed, and then calmly told me he didn't think that would ever happen. I didn't think so either, but I didn't want to take any chances with little kids and all.

I found a therapist in a nice office a few blocks from my home. Before my first visit, I was apprehensive, angst-ridden, nervous, and at the same time, excited about finally doing it. She was pleasant and listened, but I talked the whole time and told many jokes (remember, humor is my go-to thing). I told her my worries about not breaking down, even though I had been married to the love of my life and best friend, and she reassured me that not everyone had to do that. She also reassured me that there were people like me who channeled anger to get them through in the long term. She laughed at my anecdotes and funny inside stories and seemed excited to have me come back. She did ask me what I was most mad about, and I said I wanted a full and sincere apology from my ex. She asked me to write a letter to him stating all that I was mad about and what I wanted him to do, and keep the letter to myself. The writing would help me feel better and move on, and it did.

My visit the week after was again easy. I talked, and she listened and laughed. I realized then that I was OK and didn't need to keep entertaining her on my dime. Therapists do not come cheap, and while she was fine, I knew I could use the dollars on other ventures. Instead, I registered for one-on-one Spanish lessons and Latin dance classes. So my experience with therapy was short, but I have no regrets and am glad I did it. My built-in family support system was therapy. For many women going through a divorce, a therapist may be the only objective, nonjudgmental, third-party person they have, and it can be truly beneficial during the process.

A LITTLE STORY ABOUT CLUB D

During the first four or five years after my divorce, I was part of a great group of six women and two men who were single after divorce or long-term relationships. It was a great mixed bag of personalities with different divorce/breakup stories (some horrid, some funny, some almost tragic, and some drama-free), but we were all in our late thirties and early forties and single in Chicago. Boy, did we have fun! Fun in a harmless, carefree, childlike way. The ones who didn't have kids usually did a lot of the organizing and planning for our get-togethers and trips, and we would have a swell time. From movies, house parties, music in the park, museums, clubs, bars, and plays to simple pizza and game nights, we did it all. We sometimes had serious discussions, but since our work lives were so intense, we didn't take ourselves seriously and always looked forward to hanging out and just acting like kids. Most of us swore off marriage again, and most weren't interested in dating, but a few were dating (mostly the guys).

Eventually, though, the dynamics started to change as people moved on to the next phase of their lives. Some desired to couple up or remarry, and others didn't, and that was when each person had to decide what he or she wanted next. For some it was to date more, for some it was to get remarried, and for others (me) it was no marriage *ever* again.

Eventually, the group morphed into a few separate groups. From the original club D group, which is no more, we have remarrieds, happily cohabiting, dating on and off, and happily single (like me). I give this example because there are friends for different phases of life, and they are there for a season or reason. During that time, having single friends who could go out late, plan trips, or hang out last minute when my girls were with their dad made me a contented person. I could laugh at myself, laugh about dating woes and stories, and just relax with other adults. My married friends, with or without kids, were less able to fill those aspects of my life.

Another thing I learned was that it remains important to stay true to yourself and know what you want. You can be part of a group—social, church, women's group, and so on—but you still have to make your own decisions. When and if you start to want different things, you need to go for them, no hesitation, no apologies. Everyone is at different places and stages and phases, so just do *you*.

How to sustain a support system:

- Don't try to go it alone. Leaning on your support system is not a weakness. A sign of true strength is knowing when to ask for help.

- Set boundaries in a nice way.
- Be open to new types of support, and be willing to support others.
- Realize that your support system may transition and is likely to be fluid and diverse as different people fulfill different roles in your crew.
- Let your support crew know how much you appreciate all that they bring into your life. Don't take them for granted.
- Be supportive of other moms, married or single.
- Don't ditch your support system once you start dating. You may not see them as often anymore, but let them know you appreciate them. We all know women who reach out to their girlfriends in times of crisis but as soon as all is well, don't return calls. This is middle-school behavior, and as grown women, we can and should do better.

TAKE CARE OF YOURSELF

You can't pour from an empty jar. Take care of yourself first.

This one I feel needs to be emphasized repeatedly. Take care of yourself. This makes you a better mom, a better woman, and a better person to be around. There should be no guilt or stress associated with taking care of yourself. I may be contradicting myself a bit since I have said we should put the kids first, but you kind of need to put yourself first too. Many women don't even know what it means to truly take care of themselves. We are so used to caring for the kids, the spouse, the parents, the siblings, our coworkers, and our friends—everyone but ourselves. To be the best you, you have to nurture yourself.

You can take some days off if you work outside the home, and the kids don't even have to know. Take a day off to sleep, get a massage, watch reality TV, do a spa day, catch up with friends at brunch, and then pick the kids up an hour or so earlier than you normally would. That's what I call a win-win; you had me time, and the kids got to see you earlier. Time off by yourself doesn't have to cost money. It could just be alone time in your pajamas till three in the afternoon.

Discover how you need to take care of yourself. Only you know what this means. Are you an introvert or an extrovert? What calms you? Relaxes you? How do you recharge? Do you need to be alone when your energy is sapped, or do you thrive on other people's energy? You have to realize that you can't draw from an empty well, and a happy mom is a better mom. A saying I read somewhere resonated with me: "Stress is where (who) you think you should be, and peace is where (who) you are." Accepting that you are divorced and a single mom is the first step in being at peace. It doesn't mean you don't miss your married life or that you lack the desire to remarry; it means you are at peace with where things are, and you're making the best of it.

Stress is bad for your physical, mental, and emotional health, and that state of mind is not conducive to making the best decisions for yourself or the children. You are also more likely to be rash or irrational when communicating with your co-parent when you are stressed.

Vacation time is always precious and a way to connect and relax outside the day-to-day work-and-school grind. Staycations are great too, and we do that periodically just to breathe and explore all the places in our neighborhood. Many of us don't even visit our own parks and museums until we have visitors from out of town. Staycations are also a great time to chill, relax at home, do some spring cleaning, and bond with your darlings. Sitting around with hot chocolate, looking through stacks of old photos always relaxes our trio.

We love to travel and see new places, and my girls have become experts at packing for both quick weekend getaways and longer vacations. I wanted to have the disposable income to afford travel (after college savings), and this played into my decision to downsize after my divorce. I had the option of living in the big five-bedroom home with a yard, but instead I moved into a more manageable townhome with the girls. This decision was an excellent one for us, and we have had no regrets. We have taken amazing trips as a family. I have vacationed with my sisters and with my friends, but my most memorable vacations have been with my daughters. Seeing them experience new places at different ages has always been a source of joy. Our threesome vacations have taken us from Michigan to Aruba, from Miami to Paris, from Seattle to Nigeria, from Charlotte to Vancouver, from New Orleans to Toronto, from Vegas to London, and each trip was a unique experience. I am a firm believer in experiences over things, and the memories of those trips will always live in my heart. Inside jokes abound about many of our trips, and anytime I get down, I just look through albums and photos from vacations and get that instant happy jolt.

As a physician, I have to put my doctor hat on for a bit in this section about taking care of yourself. Take the time to keep up with your primary-care visits, and even if you have no medical problems, make sure you keep up with age-appropriate screening tests and vaccinations. These include mammograms at age forty and Pap smears and colonoscopies at fifty or as indicated. This is essential and nonnegotiable. Many women, single or married, put everyone else first and neglect their own health. Make time to do these screening tests. Also listen to your body, and if something feels off, see a doctor. Please also take care of your mental health as you do your physical health. Depression and anxiety are real disorders and should not be apologized for. You need to seek out and see a professional, and keep your appointments.

For many, after being married for so long and now being single, it's important to get screened for all sexually transmitted infections, like gonorrhea, chlamydia, syphilis, HIV, hepatitis B and C, and herpes. This is important as you move to postdivorce phase two for peace of mind. It also empowers you to ask that any potential partners get tested. The stakes are high, and if the last time you were dating was decades ago, you need to know the way things are out there. The prevalence of HIV in women of color is higher than for white women, and many acquire it through heterosexual intercourse. With HIV, knowledge is power, and ignorance is *not* bliss. Not getting tested can and will hurt you. There is pre-exposure prophylaxis (PREP) to prevent HIV acquisition. An early diagnosis improves prognosis and markedly decreases the risk of short- and long-term complications. Getting on effective HIV therapy improves life span, and most individuals achieve a normal life span. With walk-in STD-testing clinics and home-testing kits, there really is no excuse not to know your HIV status.

For baby boomers (those born between 1945 and 1965), doctors recommend a one-time hepatitis C test since baby boomers account for 75 percent of hepatitis C cases in the United States. Hepatitis C is curable with a short course of treatment, but it can only be cured if it's diagnosed, so get tested. If you can't find time for visits when you are well and delay until things are diagnosed late, you will not be there for the children. If you look at it this way, staying healthy and optimizing your overall health is actually putting the kids first.

Lastly, take it easy, and be kind to yourself. Relax or, as the kids say, chillax. You do not have the monopoly on sometimes messed-up or attitude-laden kids. Moms come off as extra angsty to our kids, and they can become sullen to a degree that we can't comprehend. This happens to all teenagers or preteen kids even if they aren't straddling two cultures in this increasingly tense world. That means you shouldn't personalize everything they say or do or blame it on your divorce. Kids will be bratty at times, and it's OK not to internalize everything. The last part of taking care of yourself is forgiving yourself for whatever part you played in the marriage's demise. Forgiveness is freeing.

How to take care of yourself:

- Realize that taking care of yourself *is* putting the kids first.
- Taking time out to nurture your soul is not being selfish.
- Set a standing date, such as your birthday or January of each year, to get your annual physical and mammograms. (This I learned from one of my sisters.)

This way, you are not left guessing or trying to remember if you did it.

- Find coupons or online deals to get services like massages and facials at a discounted rate.
- Tell people what you need! If it's time off, accept free babysitting in lieu of a gift on your birthday.
- Nurture your physical body in addition to your mental and spiritual health.
- Stay physically active, and try to eat well. I know that's vague, but there are tons of books, videos, and online resources for this. I especially love Zumba classes and hot yoga to recharge and rejuvenate.
- Share information about health, screening, and lifestyle changes with your friends.
- Pick your battles; your kids can't be perfect all the time, and neither can you.

KNOW YOURSELF AND STAY TRUE TO YOU

Staying true to yourself is essential to your well-being, and it allows you to stay centered and to be the best you. To stay true to yourself, you must *know* yourself. As women, we grow each day, and our life experiences make us stronger. If a woman at forty acts like a woman at twenty, that's two decades of life wasted. It may sound harsh, but it's true. You can remain young at heart and even look better than you did at twenty, but your life experiences and challenges should be reflected in how you think in your forties. You can only stay true to yourself if you are in tune with yourself. The quest to know yourself is a lifelong journey, but once you have at least a rough idea, you need to stay true to yourself.

This will help in all aspects of your life, especially navigating the world as a single mom. This means staying true to the kids; family; friends; and, most importantly, yourself.

I read somewhere that we are most balanced and at our best when our thoughts, words, and actions are all in sync. The mind-body-soul sync is at its best when what you think, what you say, and what you do all align. This is not always easy to achieve for a variety of reasons, but if you strive to do this, you will be in a happier, more Zen-like place. You can't say you want to put the kids first and then ban visits from the dad to spite him. You can't say you want to move on but then spend hours rehashing details of your marriage and ex to everyone who says hello. Go with what you feel, and align things as much as you can.

An example of staying true to yourself involves knowing when you are ready to date and why you want to date. You cannot go along with anyone else's timelines or pressures. You have to know when it's right for you. It can't be because everyone around you is dating, or your parents or sibs want you to, or the kids want a guy at the table, or it's cool to date a much younger guy, or your friends think it will make your ex jealous, and definitely not because your ex is getting married. Date when you want to, and share what your expectations are. We are grown women and don't have time for nonsense.

I thought I was ready a few years after my divorce but soon realized I was not emotionally ready to go deep. I took myself out of the dating game and will remain out until I know for sure it's what I want. Just do *you*.

A personal example of staying true to myself was knowing that I wanted to downsize when I started over. I knew that I wanted a lower mortgage and less maintenance, and

I also wanted my own place as I started version 2.0. We had a big, expensive house; a huge yard; and a play set for the girls, but I was not about trying to impress anyone or proving that I won by keeping the house. I knew I liked to travel, and the disposable income that came from downsizing would finance that need. A few people asked why I didn't keep the house, since the wife usually gets to, but I had my reasons and stood by my decision with no regrets.

Speaking of downsizing, it's easy to feel inferior, especially if you had to downsize or move across town or are the new single mom in town. Affirm your strength daily, and know that you are powerful. Your impact goes beyond your children because you are setting the course for future generations. It's not easy, but you can and are doing it. If you find yourself feeling subpar, you need to evaluate why. Is it constant or only when you are around a certain person or group of people? Do they say things that make you feel that way, or is this you feeling like you don't measure up? If it's the latter, why? If it's the former, evaluate; maybe the energy when you are with them drains or diminishes you. You may need to step away from that situation for a while. No one can diminish you or make you small. The only person who can do that is you. People can say or do things to you, but you have the right to accept or reject negative things and the power to avoid those situations. Sometimes it's because you are comparing yourself to your ex or to other women. Comparison is the killer of joy and will always make you feel inadequate and unhappy. Remember, only the great, fun, edited stuff makes it to Facebook or Instagram.

Many women, once married, find their identities tied to their husbands' statuses and achievements, and the children and their accomplishments make them feel complete. When a marriage ends, it's painful and can be downright scary. Many women feel lost, incomplete, and inadequate since their identities are so intertwined with the traditional family structure. Know that you play a vital role in the children's lives and that you will continue to do this as a single mom. This is also the time to evaluate what is important to you and why. This period, though painful, allows you to decide what, why, how, and who you spend your precious time and emotions on; I elaborate more in the next chapter on growth.

Knowing yourself involves a stop-and-check process, a complete scan of your priorities. You will need to find solitude and really look inward. It's hard to ask the tough questions, own up to our mistakes, and acknowledge our strengths. We distract ourselves with things, people, and even our wonderful children to avoid looking within. Ask yourself the tough questions, and be ready for the answers.

Part of the growth process and knowing yourself is the no-grumbling zone. When we grumble constantly, it gives our negative thoughts and words power and could quickly become the norm. Have you noticed that when you grumble and whine, it becomes a habit? It's easy to do. Whining can make you feel better temporarily and sometimes gets you attention, but in the long run, it's draining, both for you and for those who have the misfortune of listening to you all the time. You don't always have to give power to thoughts that come through your mind, and sometimes letting those go is the way to move on and be positive.

So why do we grumble or scowl so much? The myth of the happy ending is why many women, single or married, mom or not, may feel unhappy or unfulfilled. When you have a fixed, ideal concept of a happy ending, you find yourself always longing for that and missing out on the happiness that is present today. For some women, the happy ending is the husband, big house, and kids, so, when divorce happens, the happy ending is ruined. They spend all their time mourning that or desperately, frantically trying to recreate that ideal on a self-imposed artificial timeline. There's nothing wrong with wanting to remarry and have all that, but you don't want to miss out on the joys in your present as you go after your ideal. It's hard to accept sometimes, but your ideal may not be your happy ending, and living in the present allows you to be open to alternative paths in life.

We have the proper goals for our lives when we can experience joy in every circumstance. You can't will joy or choose to be joyful; it flows from the inside. It flows when you value every day you are alive and healthy and consider the privilege you have been given to raise the next generation. We have been blessed with so much responsibility and have the power to shape the lives of the next generation, and I do consider that a great privilege.

Recently, my church pastor gave an example of two basketball players on a team. One player absolutely loves the game and wants to enjoy each game and get better, and the other just wants the fame of being the star of the team. It's clear that they have very different attitudes toward losses and when they don't play as much or as well as usual. The player whose goal is fame is selfish, wants more playing time, and is distraught by a loss. He might not do his best work unless there is a scout or at least adoring fans around. The player who loves the game plays unselfishly; wants to learn and grow from losses; plays his best each time he steps on the court, even during practice; and is glad for the opportunity to play each time. You want to be the second player—joyful about being a mom, learning from your ups and downs, and being thankful for each day you have.

I'll give an example from a world closer to mine of two medical students, both smart. You have one medical student who just wants to shine on his or her cases when the lead attending is around versus the other student who takes time to go back to the wards after rounds, listens and learns from others, and knows that nothing learned is lost in medicine. That second student is well-rounded and will be equipped to take on a variety of patients in the future. I know everyone reading this wants the student who loves medicine and learning as much as possible taking care of their moms. No time or experience shared with your children is wasted even when it seems basic and unglamorous. Our biggest aha moments and bonding sometimes happen during these times. The lesson here is to embrace and appreciate your circumstances and the privilege of raising children, even when it's not all glam, and joy will flow from inside.

How to stay true to yourself:

- Find solitude, and conduct periods of introspection. It's hard to do but necessary.
- Ask tough questions of yourself, and be ready to deal with the emotions involved.
- Meditate.
- Pray for wisdom.
- Write down the words that describe you, and see if they match the way friends describe you.

- Know that no one else can be you, and you should not be anyone else.
- Strive to have your thoughts, words, and actions align.
- Avoid comparing yourself or your lifestyle to others. Remember that Facebook and Instagram posts are only a snapshot in time and everyone is putting their best out there!
- Be authentic. Have the courage to be yourself.
- Just do *you*!

DO NOT RUSH INTO ANYTHING AND NEVER SETTLE

Know your worth, and own and appreciate the awesome you! There are as many reasons why women need to hear this as there are reasons women settle for suboptimal choices. I know it can be lonely, and companionship is great, but know your reasons for wanting to date or remarry, and make sure they are the right ones. Many women rush into the next relationship because they think "it's what you do," "sounds like a plan," or "my ex moved on." Or they think that if they wait, they may not find anyone, or they're getting old and no one wants single moms, so they should take the first offer that comes along. None of these are good reasons to be in a relationship or remarry. Realize that being alone and being lonely are different things. Alone, you can be alive, vibrant, and content, and you can be in a relationship or marriage and still be lonely. A friend once told me that static did not mean stagnant, and while you are single, you are growing. Do the next relationship on your own timeline, and when you are ready, you will know. It can be intimidating, scary, and angst-ridden if you've been out of the dating game for a while, but you've got this.

In the spirit of sisterhood and full disclosure, I wanted to share information about my dating life. In the first two or three years postdivorce, dating was a no-no, and my resolve was never again! After being asked many times when I thought I would be ready to date, my standard default answer was that I would consider dating after my baby left for college. That was far enough away, usually got people to stop asking, and seemed liked a great timeline to me. I know some may question why I felt this way for so long, but it's important to realize that we all have different timelines. My divorce was too raw, my heart too fragile, and my driving focus was to protect my children. I had no interest or desire to date, and since one-night stands had never been my thing, I was fine to just let that part of my life go into hibernation mode.

Between years four and eight, I did date a few times. The dates were organic, not sought out or set up, and arose based on common interests. In each case, I remained protective of my heart. I sheltered my kids and strived to keep the relationships on my own terms, needing a lot of space. My ideal dating set up was to hang out a few times a month (two to four, maximum), live in different parts of the city or preferably different states, and to never discuss anything more serious than that. No talk of moving in together or spending more time together and definitely not marriage. In retrospect, I realize that I was in a selfish place. I felt like if I didn't want marriage or more kids or need the financial support, why would I want someone else to listen to and worry about?

The longer I was single and doing it all, the more I felt like any additional person to care about was an unnecessary burden. I considered relationships a lot of work, with me giving my time and space and not necessarily seeing what I got out of it. As a planner, nurturer, and caregiver, I didn't have the time or interest in having another person on my schedule. The kids and my career were full-time jobs, and anything else was work.

This, to anyone reading this now, is a clear indication that I was still hurting and had set up barriers. I wanted so much to protect my heart but convinced myself that this was the rational, clear-minded way any adult woman should do this. I didn't judge anyone who was eager to pair up again or even get married, but I couldn't understand why I would want to do that. I couldn't risk having my heart broken, and more importantly, I didn't want my daughters to get their hearts broken.

These men were good men, not perfect (neither was I). They enjoyed spending time with me, were kind to me, and treated me with utmost respect. In each situation, things got more serious, and they wanted more of my time and space and heart. That was the end of the relationship each time, and I realized three things:

1. I was in a selfish place and not ready to share my life in a romantic relationship.
2. Relationships evolve, and if you're not ready to evolve, you're not ready to be in a relationship.
3. It wasn't fair to anyone, and yes, men do have feelings.

I had a technical, uncompromising, my-rules-only setup around these relationships and was not willing to give more. With that realization, I took myself out of the dating game and have stayed firmly out of it for years.

Relationships require compromises, and until I am in a place where I want one and am willing to compromise and share my life, I am staying firmly single. I am making use of all that extra time to get things done; learn new skills; write a book; and enjoy my children, family, and friends. Now that I am on my way to becoming an empty nester next year with even more free time, who knows what happens next. Writing this book has been cathartic, even therapeutic, and that bodes well for the future.

"You're ready to be back in the dating game when you don't feel like you need a man, but you feel like you want one," writes Sharon McKenna, author of *Sex and the Single Mom*. Yes, you're not as young as you were the first time, but you are now a more mature, sexier woman who knows what she wants. If you are not in it for kids or money, then you are set. You don't have to settle, and that's a great thing.

So what happens when you're ready and it's time to get back out there? Yikes! I have no tips for this. You're on your own! I'm still trying to figure out when I'll be ready to get back out there. Thankfully, there are many groups, books, online sites, and apps on how to get back out there, how to date, and how to land the man. One thing for sure is that wherever you are in the world, when you hear about people dating, especially in their forties and fifties, it's unreal how much they have to say. There are tons of stories—hilarious stories; horror stories; outrageous stories; and cute, over-the-top romantic stories—so you can make it as much fun as you want it to be. As you reenter the dating world, there may be some new norms and trends that you're not familiar with, such as sexting, nude pics, and crotch shots (ugh), which you may find either thrilling or not so thrilling. Don't be pressured to keep up because everyone is doing it, even women your age. You're not a teenager, and peer pressure should not be a thing anymore. This is a gentle reminder to know yourself, and stay true to you.

Your safety is paramount, and it's essential to always let a friend know where you are and who you are out with. You are a grown woman, so there's no need to be undercover or on the sly about your dates. If you are out, let someone know. And do use common sense, and trust your gut. These gut instincts are real and can be lifesaving. Your intuition is a God-given gift. Use it!

For me, watching the Lifetime and Lifetime Movies channels has made me borderline paranoid. Every guy on there seems to be a psycho or sexual predator, and every new friend or neighbor usually has a weird, twisted revenge plot. I know it's not real life, but I must say, it's made me extra cautious and ready to stay home forever. If you do venture out, be safe.

There is no need to rush into anything even though as women, wanting to feel whole again, we sometimes rush into relationships that are not right for us and stay in them for the same reasons. This is your chance to critically evaluate yourself and what's out there, and take your time to find the right fit. In health care, surgeries fall into the emergent, urgent, or elective category, and for most emergent surgeries, you don't get to choose your surgeon. You pray for the best as you are wheeled into surgery. For cosmetic surgery, which is elective, you get personal and professional recommendations; set up consultations with a few surgeons; and look up their ratings, complication rates, and outcomes, and then you plan the surgery, get your mind right, and do it. You don't just settle for the first surgeon who sees you. As a single mom, you have time, choices, and options, and you should always exercise your power and right to choose if, when, how, and who to couple with.

In this next section, I want to address what I think is the most important topic, which is protecting your children. They are young, naïve, and yours to protect. Take time before you expose them to the men or women in your life. Try not to make them a part of the revolving door, if you have one. They do get emotionally invested, especially if Dad is not involved, and you don't want their tiny hearts to break. Listen to them. If they have complaints, anxiety, or mood changes or if your gut says something is off, then pause and listen. Don't get so swept up in your romance that you ignore your children. It may be nothing, or it may be something. Err on the side of caution; assume that it is something, and listen, investigate, and evaluate. There will be other men if things don't work out, but your children only have one mother. I cannot overemphasize this issue because sometimes, single moms make decisions that they think may be for the greater good. Sometimes it's for financial reasons, sometimes it's for security reasons, sometimes it's to fit in, and other times it's to fill a void. Whatever your reasons are, please remember that the kids are to be protected *always*. I'm not saying that all men are predators or abusers—in fact, the vast majority of men are not—but when you have strangers around your children, realize that they don't have the same obligation to put your children's interests first.

In addition, there are crazies out there who prey on vulnerable single moms just to get around their children. A young girl or boy may not know that it's not appropriate to be touched in a certain way, or a teenage girl missing her dad may get too close to Mom's boyfriend. I cannot tell you how many stories of abuse from moms' boyfriends I have heard in my professional life, and no matter how old these women are, those memories are vivid, and they hurt. In many instances, they have forgiven their moms, but they can never forget. This can happen to boys as well. Abuse, especially from someone brought into your life by your mom, has damaging, long-term effects on the kids. It affects how they see themselves, who they choose to be with, how loved they feel, and how secure they feel. This is not a trivial issue, and it's one you should pay attention to. Many of the unpleasant children-of-divorce statistics out there are closely tied to these issues. Between the stories I have heard and Lifetime television, there were very real reasons I chose not to date when the kids were young, and when I did eventually date, it was with all senses and intuition on alert for anything off.

How to date when you are ready:

- Let your friends know you are ready. In the old-fashioned, pre–dating app world, blind dates and friend setups worked.
- Go on those apps and sites and figure out what works for you. There are tons to choose from, and many are free. My kids have tried to convince me to get on Match.com, Plenty of Fish, ChristianMingle, or OurTime. (They think I am old.)

- Continue to do you, grow, and explore. Be open to people you meet at the gym, yoga, art class, language class, travel, and school events. Be careful with people in the workplace—I don't think that's always a great idea.
- Own your awesomeness and never feel like dating you is a favor. You are divorced, you have kids, *and* this makes you fabulous.
- Let a friend know where you are and who you are with. Set your location device. Send a selfie with your date. No underground moves. You're a grown woman.
- Take time before you introduce your kids to your new partner. Don't make them part of your revolving door. You may not be emotionally invested, but kids can get attached quickly.
- Protect your children, and listen to their concerns. Even if they don't say anything, be sure to listen and look, and do not mute your intuition. It's there to protect you and your loved ones and should never be ignored.
- Have fun, and ignore my paranoid musings about Lifetime television.

GROW, REFINE, GROW!

Wholeness is possible only via the coexistence of opposites. In order to know the light, we must experience the dark.

—CARL JUNG

Use the postdivorce as a time for personal growth. It is a fact that two seemingly opposing perspectives can be true at the same time. The dark time of a divorce could also be the bright start of personal growth. Think of this as a time to press the reset button, recharge, and restart. There are few times in life when we get to stop and reflect. I know we reflect often and sometimes daily, but if we are brutally honest with ourselves, the only time we stop, take stock, and evaluate ourselves is when all is not well. Think about situations in your work life. You may have had unease, dissatisfaction, or angst, but it's what you know, and you become complacent and live with the chronic discontent. Most times, you do nothing to reflect on why you feel this way and how to remedy that. When you are forced to find a new job due to downsizing, you stop and reflect. You figure out your strengths, how to work on your weaknesses, the industry standards, how to position yourself, and how to clearly articulate what you want in the next job.

Think of your divorce in those terms. It's a hard stop, an opportunity to reboot and restart version 2.0. If you approach this tough time that way and think of it as a growth opportunity, you will not only survive it, you will thrive.

When the growth happens, it does not happen by accident. It is intentional. Just like we are intentional about so many things, like getting the kids into the best schools and finding the best sales at Thanksgiving, you should make this growth mind-set something you strive for. I'm talking about growth as a woman, a mom, and a professional to become what you know you can be.

There is no point living as a single mom like you're in limbo, waiting for life to start again. Where you are now is your life now, and you need to live it to the fullest. If you do this, you will thrive instead of barely surviving or just being there. You need to be present and engaged. You only have one life to live, and you can't be a passive spectator. You are the star. By not being present, you are saying that life is only worth living with a spouse, and that the kids don't matter as much. Children thrive and grow when you are thriving. Growth during this time is important, and you should think of all the positives that come with having the time to reset and reboot.

One of the areas in which I grew was in finances. Any day, any time you wake me up from sleep, I know my investment portfolio, bank-account balances, mortgage rate and balance, escrow, credit score, fidelity college funds, pension-plan updates, and best credit cards for what rewards. I subscribe to *Money* and other investor magazines and track the stock market on my phone. Wow, you're thinking, who is this maven doctor who knows finance?

Well, it wasn't always like that. It was far from that. I knew nothing about finances the day I walked into my divorce attorney's office. I was a joke—a pathetic joke! She asked me a bunch of simple questions: How much do you make? How much does your husband make? Who does your taxes? Do you have investment properties? What life-insurance policies do you have? How much is in the college accounts? These were simple enough questions, but I didn't know the answers to any of them, including how much money I made. After the sixth question, she politely told me I needed to do some homework and gave me a written list of questions she wanted answers to by the next meeting.

This was me—a fully functioning, kick-ass medical doctor who ran my home and was taking no prisoners at work but knew nothing about my finances. It was pathetic, but my lawyer reassured me it was not unusual. She had seen many couples in which one partner did all the money stuff, and the other took care of the home, kids, and school stuff. Yes, one of you may have an affinity for the financial aspects, but that is no excuse for the other one giving up all the power and being a passive observer. Learn some money stuff too. Stay informed, and know where things are and who is managing what. I had to at crunch time, and I am a better person for it.

Understand that things could be worse or get worse. This is hard to believe sometimes when you are in the throes of your divorce, but it could get worse. You could be a celebrity with every part of your breakup publicized, and the minute your ex is dating, it's on social media. Or your ex could move from the city back to your suburb, a few blocks from you with his new family, and his stepchild could attend your kids' school. You could have to see his new wife at every school event and fundraiser you volunteer at. That was me, but it made me better, not bitter. The children are watching and develop their emotional IQ through cues from you. Emotional maturity comes at a different pace and rate for everyone, and mine clearly accelerated during this phase.

"Grow each day" is a motto of mine. Learning a new word or a new skill or finding a new app makes me joyful. The thrill of reading about a new disease or syndrome makes me giddy. I like to go to bed each night smarter than I was in the morning. Anyone who knows me knows that I hunger for new knowledge and believe that nothing learned is wasted. This makes every day exciting and every interaction a potential learning opportunity. If you think about it, with every interaction, you learn something about yourself, another person, a situation, or just life. Resolve to learn something new every day. If you make it a mission, it will happen. Being a lifelong learner is an asset that will help in all spheres of your life.

How to do grow, refine, grow:

- Reflect on the marriage, and identify ways in which you may have contributed to its demise. This is not to say that you should blame yourself or criticize yourself. This is about going deep, reflecting, and being honest. If there is nothing you could have done better, then skip this step.
- Reassure yourself that all will be well, and know that it will be. Stepping out each day, confident about your growth, will make you whole.

- Revitalize yourself in many ways. Physical, mental, emotional, and spiritual revitalization is the way to grow during your reboot for version 2.0.
- Renew your mind and your interests in things you loved as a kid, a teenager, or a single adult before you became a mom. Find joy in doing those things, and watch yourself flourish and bloom like a kid again.
- Invest in yourself. No knowledge is wasted.
- Replenish your stores in whatever way you recharge.
- Disengage from people or situations that drag you down or waste your time.
- Realize that falling forward means you can get back up after you have been knocked down.
- Never forget to pay it forward. Every day that you move on as a divorced woman, another woman is just starting the process or thinking about it.

CHAPTER 6

MORE RANDOM MUSINGS

I HEARD YOU THE FIRST TIME

JUST LIKE PREGNANCY—when everyone has an opinion and people ask personal, intrusive questions; touch your bump; and argue with you about the gender of your unborn child—divorce makes people talkative. They want to talk about you and to you. Even people who are not close to you feel obliged to comment on your situation, offer unsolicited advice, or just plain pry into your business.

Some things single moms hear a lot and are sometimes not in the mood for:

"I feel bad for you."
Me: Please don't! It doesn't help anything and can drag me down on a day when I'm feeling really great! Instead say, "You are amazing. How can I help?"

"I don't know how you do it all."
Me: It's hard and sometimes a real challenge or struggle.
Instead say, "You are amazing. How can I help?"

"I am so jealous of you."
Me: Are you honestly saying you want my life? Or do you like the fact that I can date? Or do you think it makes me feel better to hear you say that?
Instead say, "You look amazing, and you are doing a fantastic job!"

"Are you dating?"
Me: This is a very common one I heard and continue to hear. It's usually the second or third thing women say after they hear you're divorced. It's almost like you're missing a part or are broken if you aren't part of a couple. It's a combination of trying to gauge the prospects of a forty-something-year-old single mom and living vicariously through me.
Instead say, "You look amazing, and anyone would be lucky to get to share your life."

"Don't you miss having sex?"
Me: WTF? Never appropriate unless you are BFFs or playing truth or dare.
Instead say, "You are amazing and look amazing."

"I wish I had all that free time like you do."
Me: Really? Free time? Yes, if you are fortunate to have a co-parent who has the kids on weekends, you do have time to do things you enjoy, but the rest of the time is a lot of work.
Instead say, "You are amazing, and I am happy you get time to enjoy the things you like."

"Husbands are overrated."
Me: It does not make me feel better if that was the intention.
Instead say, "You look amazing."

"If I got divorced, I would never remarry."
Me: OK, good for you. All you get from me is a smile and a nod because that's all you will get from me.
Instead say, "You are amazing, you look amazing, and like I said, you are amazing."

What single moms I've spoken to miss most about being married:

- A steady date to events like dinner parties, movies, church, and neighborhood or work events
- Not always having to be both the good cop and the bad cop with the kids
- Anniversary dates and romantic holidays
- Having someone to share their work angst with at the end of the day
- Throwing dinner parties and hanging with other couples
- Regular sex (but this did not make the top ten that often)
- Having someone to take care of the car repairs and maintenance stuff around the home, like taking out the garbage
- Traveling with the kids on family vacations
- The big house, especially if their lifestyles have changed
- Holiday traditions

- Having backup when a kid is ill
- Having someone to pamper them when they are ill or just need a little TLC.

Things that will kill your joy and make you a miserable mom and a bitter woman:

- Comparing yourself to others
  The grass is never greener on the other side.

- Not growing from the pain and remaining stagnant
  Staying stagnant or living in the past robs you of true growth.

- Waiting to get excited or energized when things get better
  You only have one life to live; be present and make the best of it.

- Constantly blaming your divorce for why things are not perfect
  If your marriage had been perfect, it wouldn't have ended.

- Not loving and appreciating yourself
  If you don't love you, you will only attract people who don't value or appreciate you.

- Feeling like you need someone else to bring you joy
  True happiness comes from within; others just enhance it.

- Not being true to yourself or wanting to be like someone else
  Authenticity is the courage to be your true self. It's a very attractive quality.

FINDING THE POSITIVE IN EVERYTHING

I chose twelve examples because I wrote this book twelve years after my divorce.

1. **Sleeping alone.** There's no need to share covers, no snoring, no fighting over temperature control, and you can eat in bed. You can make the most of your space until the right person comes along. Also, there's more space for kids to snuggle even when they are teens or older. (Mine still do!) Caveat—you can get so comfortable with your space that sharing becomes a major issue. (This is me.)

2. **No one to talk to at night.** Get productive. (My laptop was in bed with me for the first three years, and I published quite a bit.) You can journal or, better yet, catch up on Bravo shows and Lifetime television for women. With Netflix and Amazon Prime, the sky's the limit. You could also just get more sleep. It's good for the skin.

3. **Lack of steady sex.** If you're being honest, it probably wasn't always steady, and often your ex wanted to and you were soooo tired. My answer to this is exercise, yoga, and a fabulous vibrator until you're ready to get back out there.

4. **Dinners without a spouse.** You get to decide what everyone eats, and you don't have to check with anyone. The kids are yours to feed—that's it! You also learn to dine alone when the kids are with Dad. I have always enjoyed personal time, but if you don't, this is the time to grow that part of you.

5. **Traveling alone with the kids**. You get to decide where and when you travel. That's fun. According to Yahoo! Travel, one of the trips you should take before you die is a solo trip. This could be the one you do when kids are with their dad. People are also kinder to you and more willing to help and tolerate screaming, bratty kids if you are a single mom. Milk it while you can.

6. **Can't afford as many vacations**. Figure out ways to create amazing staycations. Explore parts of your city you only visit when you have out-of-town guests. Volunteer with the kids locally. This is an opportunity for the kids to give back and to realize that there are always people less fortunate than they are. Remember, we can spin the narrative any way we want, and kids look to us as they interpret situations.

7. **Income issues**. You get to exercise parts of your brain that may have been dormant when you were married. Overseeing finances and budgeting can be hard if you've never done it (in my case, I took care of the kids, and he took care of our finances), but trust me, that's an area for growth. Now I know all about investing, market trends, and retirement plans, and I feel like a well-rounded woman.

8. **Miss the kids when they are away with Dad**. This is a good problem to have. If this is happening to you, it means your co-parent has an active role in the children's lives and spends time with them. In my case, he does, and I have had days or entire weekends when I moped or missed them. Instead of wondering how they are doing, what he's buying them,

or if they're hanging with the new girlfriend, think of that time as a well-deserved staycation. As moms (single or married), we hardly get protected time for ourselves, so when you do, please enjoy yourself guilt-free. Read a book, get your nails done, go to the spa, go to the gym, go shopping (if you can afford to), hang out with friends, or take a vacation. If these times with Dad are regular and scheduled, you could take classes. Over the decade, I have taken dance classes, language classes, and art classes; joined book clubs; traveled with friends; and volunteered. Next up is improv classes and becoming a certified Zumba instructor. Talk about making use of time!

9. **Had to downsize.** That's OK if that's what makes financial sense. It's your life—don't compare yourself to anyone else. The bonuses include lower heating and air-conditioning bills (Chicago extremes!) and less space to store junk.

10. **Don't have time to do anything for myself.** I agree that time is tight, especially when you are taking on the jobs of Mom and Dad as well as possibly working outside the home. It's especially worse if your co-parent is not involved, and you don't get the time off I mentioned above. That said, you can always make time. Look at your day, and see where you can carve out an hour for yourself before bed—if not daily, then two to three times per week. You can get older kids to help out or share sitters with a neighbor or friend. Be creative. We always are!

11. **Broken traditions.** This can be a real heartbreaker, but only if you let it. While the traditions are hard, especially the ones around holidays, this is the time to make new memories and create new traditions. Sometimes the children even enjoy doing things twice around the holidays. We never miss putting up the Christmas tree with the radio blaring carols, wearing our goofy hats, and sipping hot chocolate.

12. **Dating again is scary.** This is true, and yes, you are older. However, you are wiser and sexier, and you know who you are and what you want. This could be phase two or a fabulous plan B.

FAVORITE QUOTES AND WHAT THEY MEAN TO ME

Happiness is not about what the world gives you.
Happiness is how you think about what the world
gives you.

—MO GAWDAT

This helps you realize that happiness and fun are not the same things. Make your lowest point the zero point, and start to build on it, resolving to make each day better.

Comparison is the thief of all joy.

—THEODORE ROOSEVELT

We are often OK until we start comparing ourselves to others. Looking at other people's vacations, pictures, college choices, and Facebook fun can make you feel worse. Realize that people only post the good stuff. Those posts are a snapshot in time, and everyone has good, bad, and ugly times.

The most common way people give up their power
is by thinking they don't have any.

—ALICE WALKER

You are a strong woman, powerful and accomplished, and that is more than enough. You have power in your words and actions and should never give that power away.

Yesterday is not ours to recover, but tomorrow is ours to win or lose.

—LYNDON B. JOHNSON

You cannot change the past, but you can definitely frame and decide how you go forward.

Attitude is a little thing that makes a big difference.

—WINSTON CHURCHILL

Being positive is a choice. It comes easier to some than others, but it can be achieved. Our kids look to us for cues, and our attitude in the postdivorce phase makes a big difference.

There is no such thing as a perfect parent, so just be a real one.

—SUE ATKINS

We do our best, and leave the rest. It's time to let go of the guilt around the divorce and our shortcomings. Our children value quality time with us, and authenticity is the key.

> *Behind every young child who believes in himself is a parent who believed first.*
>
> —MARTIN L. JACOBSON

This one speaks for itself.

> *Counteract conflict by connection and communicating calmly.*
>
> —KRISTY LEE

While this is hard to do in many cases with your co-parent, it is essential to keep the peace as much as you can in order to raise well-adjusted children.

CHAPTER 7

THRIVING AFTER DIVORCE

FINAL THOUGHTS

THE GIRLS ARE thriving and acing life, but there are times when I still wonder if I could have done better. They are confident, compassionate, creative, and courageous young women, yet I still have bouts of guilt over our marriage ending and the roles they were thrust into as children of divorce. While the course of their lives may not have been dramatically different, I know there are ways our divorce affected them. I try not to dwell on those things, and when those thoughts come up, I dig deep and switch to positivity mode.

I know they missed out on having a block full of ready-made play dates and school friends when we moved after the divorce. Growing up, I played soccer and table tennis, cycled, and climbed trees with girls and boys, and I was comfortable around boys in a casual, nonsexual way. It demystified the girls-boys thing, and I felt it was important for my girls to have that. Our town-home complex, while beautiful, did not have other kids. They were the only kids in the seven-home complex, which was very different from our old block that had lots of kids to play with. I felt bad that their childhood was altered by our decision as adults. I worried that the easy, casual friendships that come from growing up on a block filled with other kids was taken away from them at the ages of six and seven. They did make friends and had a fun childhood, but it was more work to arrange playdates. On the positive side, this has made them loyal friends who value the friendships they have.

My girls also did not get to see the daily dynamics of a marital relationship. The romance, the stressful periods, the etiquette around discipline, household duties and roles, the arguments, dinnertime discussions, and highs and lows that come in any marriage. I worry that since they were so young when we got divorced, they might be ill prepared for conflict management and compromise in relationships or marriage. I worry that they may take the easy way out and walk away if issues arise. Then I remind myself that we talk all the time. We talk about how relationships are not always perfect, and they take work and commitment. TV and movies are snapshots, and Mom and Dad are always there if and when questions come up. They see my siblings and their spouses, and my parents spend a lot of time with us, so they do see what love, commitment, and respect in marriage look like.

I also used to worry that since I made being a single mom with a full-time career look relatively easy, they would think that was the ideal or that marriage was unnecessary. As they got older, I realized this was not the case. They respect and admire my resolve to make the most of each day, but they also want and dream of marriage. They don't idolize my life. Instead they know I live and enjoy each day and that their lives are theirs to live. They are at the age when they are in love with love, and more than anything, they want Mom to date and get married again. They want the thrill and excitement of new love for me and for themselves.

I am the first to admit that while things went as well as could be expected for the most part, there were things I discovered later that would have helped along the way. In the spirit of sisterhood and full disclosure, here's a list of things I could have done better.

1. Asking for and accepting offered help. Needing help is not a weakness, and refusing help when you need it is a problem with your pride and ego. Always being self-sufficient does not make you perfect. When you realize this, it is a sign of growth and maturity.

2. Taking time to mourn the loss of my marriage. I did not do this and instead channeled my energy (anger) into action and doing. I prided myself on multitasking and doing everything without missing a day of work or skipping a beat. I think this affected how long it took me to want to be vulnerable again and to open myself up to a lasting relationship. Twelve years later, I may just be getting there.

3. Feeling guilty for free time without the kids. You need to care for yourself and refresh and nourish your soul. You will be a better mom and woman, and the kids can only benefit from the better you. No guilt anymore.

4. Closing off a lot of relationships to avoid any issues with married friends. I took this to an extreme and avoided many people for so long. Sure, there are people you don't feel comfortable being around and should avoid, but casting a net across all marrieds is not the right thing to do. Over time I started to reintegrate into that group, and it's been great.

5. Trying to be supermom. It's hard enough being a woman, a black woman, a black woman physician, a mom in any society…and then add in raising girls as a single mom—*it's a lot.* Some things will have to give, and that's OK, as long as the kids are not harmed and understand why some decisions must be made. Once I accepted this, I got into a different, more Zen-like space. I had no problem pulling the single-mom card when I told my darlings that they couldn't do travel soccer, could do only one activity each season, or had to be on the same team so I didn't spend my entire weekend in the cold, watching soccer.

Blessings can be direct or indirect. While divorce was not in my plan, and I envisioned a long, happy, till-death-do-us-part marriage, the reality is that my divorce was an indirect blessing. The woman, daughter, sister, mother, and friend I am today is a result of the refinement that came with my divorce. No matter how I spin it, I would not be the person I am today, and I value, nurture, and celebrate who I am today. I was speaking with a friend (a single mom) recently about how well our college freshmen seemed to have adjusted to college life and the independence of being away from home. She made a statement that resonated with me. She said, "What did you expect? The kids see you, know the struggles, admire your strength and resilience, and get out there, ready to take on the world." This, my dear friends, is what it's all about. The ability to raise well-adjusted, independent children despite the issues of divorce is what it's all about.

For me, it's been a ride, and I can say that I have come out on the other side a refined, finely tuned version of myself. I have no idea what the next decade holds for me, but I am excited about the future. I am thankful to God for where I am and know that the best is yet to come. Who knows if this good-book-and-a-glass-of-wine girl may eventually venture into serious dating or even remarriage? If I do, it may be the content for the decade-after-the-decade book in 2027.

Every day is a blessing and an opportunity to grow and influence the lives of our children and others. I consider motherhood a privilege and remain thankful in all things.

Appreciate this time, consider it a time of growth, and use it to emerge a stronger, better, finer version of yourself—the 2.0 model. Go through this process and emerge better, not bitter. Get out there with undaunted courage and a boldness that is humble yet fierce. You've got this, girl!

TWELVE DIVORCE AND PARENTING BOOKS YOU MAY ENJOY

Adele Fisher and Elaine Mazlish. *How to Talk So Kids Will Listen & Listen So Kids Will Talk.* (Rawson: Wade Publishers, 1980).
(I like this one because it was easy to read, practical, and insightful.)

Harry H. Harrison Jr. *1001 things Every Teen Should Know before They Leave Home.* (Thomas Nelson Publishers, 2007)
(Funny, practical, real-life tips, and I learned a lot too!)

Nina Tassler with Cynthia Littleton. *What I Told My Daughter: Lessons from Leaders on Raising the Next Generation of Empowered Women.* (New York: ATRIA Books, 2016).
(A must-read for all women. Great advice for girls and women of all ages.)

Beth Kobliner. *Make Your Kid a Money Genius (Even If You're Not)* (Simon and Schuster, 2017)
(Packed with information, yet easy to follow. We can never be too early when it comes to teaching financial responsibility.)

The 100 Most Important Bible Verses for Mothers (W publishing group, 2006)
(Packed with verses that touch whatever aspect of life we are going through. It's a go-to for me.)

What I Know Now. Letters to My Younger Self. Edited by Ellyn Spragins. (Broadway Books, 2006).
(I liked the short letters from powerful women. A lot to learn and teach our young girls.)

JoAnn Deak, PhD, with Teresa Barker. *Girls Will Be Girls. Raising Confident and Courageous Daughters.* (New York: Hyperion Books, 2002).
(This is one of my all-time favorites! Every page is packed with insight, practical examples, and solutions. To have strong, confident women, we must raise confident girls.)

Sheila Ellison. *The Courage to Be a Single Mother: Becoming Whole Again After Divorce.* (HarperCollins, 2000).
(One of the books I read early in my divorce. I found it helpful, and it allowed me to keep things in perspective.)

Penny Kaganoff and Susan Spano. *Women on Divorce: A Bedside Companion.* (A Harvest Book, 1995).
(I read this a year or two after my divorce, and it was eye opening. Reading about how other women processed and went through their divorces was insightful. It was also valuable in helping me realize that no matter how bad things look, it could be much worse.)

Constance Ahrons, PhD. *The Good Divorce: Keeping Your Family Together When Your Marriage Comes Apart.* (HarperCollins, 1995).
(This was one of the first books I read once the divorce process was initiated. My drive was to protect the kids and minimize any damage to them. It was given to me by my coworker, now friend, who was going through a divorce. I would recommend it any day.)

Suzanne Riss and Jill Sockwell. *The Optimist's Guide to Divorce.* (Workman publishing co, 2016)
(I read this just a few weeks ago and loved the premise and the idea of the book: two women starting a neighborhood club to

support each other and other women going through a divorce. The book was insightful and practical and covered a wide variety of issues related to divorce.)

Majorie Savage. *You're on Your Own (But I'm Here if You Need Me). Mentoring Your Child During the College Years.* (Fireside Books, 2003).
(This is a new one I bought a year ago as my older daughter headed to college. It's a must-read for this stage of life, and I have recommended it to a few other moms this year.)

And of course...
Stephen R. Covey. *The 7 Habits of Highly Effective People: Powerful Lessons in Personal Change.* (New York: Simon and Schuster, 1989, 2004).

ACKNOWLEDGMENTS

To God, my heavenly father, who gives me the strength to do all things.

To my parents, Abiodun and Adeyinka Falusi, who raised me to be God fearing, confident, and compassionate. Through your examples, you instilled in us the importance of family, always striving to do our best, giving back, and remaining thankful in all circumstances. You have always been there for us, and we are eternally grateful.

To my siblings Titilope, Anuolu, Ebun, and Ibukun, you are the best anyone could ask for. The girls love you to bits and look up to you all. You inspire me daily and love me unconditionally, and your encouragement, advice, and unwavering support are appreciated and will never be taken for granted.

To my sister-friend Katayoun—you exemplify what *friend* truly means, and my family and I are grateful to have you in our lives.

To Stella, our nanny-turned-aunt. The girls and I love you, and I will be forever grateful for how you love and care for my darlings like they are yours.

To our church family. The church remains a strong foundation and anchor for our lives. The instructional and inspiring sermons renew my soul and equip me to face the challenges life may throw at me.

To my close friends who stood by me through thick and thin—your friendship is valued.

To all the mothers out there, single and married, thank you for being you. You are strong, powerful, and fabulous. You are molding and shaping the next generation, and you should never forget how awesome you are.

And to my daughters, Tosin and Funmi, my blessings from God, who teach me daily the meaning of unconditional love, I thank you. Our journey together inspired me to write this book. Your strong spirits, forgiving hearts, compassionate souls, and funny, goofy personalities make me happy and fulfilled, and I consider myself privileged to be your mother.

Thanks for reading. I would love to hear from you!
email- tfal6812@gmail.com
website-www.thedecadeafter.com
facebook/thedecadeafter.com
twitter @thedecadeafter

Our Trio-The early years

Our trio 2015-2017

Our trio with my family

SPARE...ME

Sisterhood, Persistence, Awareness, Recognition, Empowerment
Founders: Katayoun Rezai and Toyin Falusi (KRTF)

SPAREme launched in 2017 as an initiative to empower women of all ages.

I try to incorporate everything about **SPARE me** into my daily life. The **SPARE me** motto helped keep me motivated through the process of writing this book.

Sisterhood—My motivation to write this book was to have an opportunity to share tips and positive lessons with other women.

Persistence—That's what it takes to complete a book. Some days, writing was easy; other times, it was really hard.

Awareness—Knowing that we all have different separation and divorce scenarios, but we all want the best for our children and for ourselves.

Recognition—Recognizing that women rock, and single moms are exceptional, doing great things (big and small) daily.

Empowerment—Empowering women of all ages or marital status to be positive and grow daily and, no matter how dire or difficult the circumstances, to get better, not bitter.

For more information about SPARE...me and to read our blogs, visit our website and like us on Facebook.
Website: w-spare.me
Facebook.com/w.spare

CPSIA information can be obtained
at www.ICGtesting.com
Printed in the USA
LVHW090737270420
654496LV00008B/2264